AN INTELLIGENT PERSON'S GUIDE TO EDUCATION

OTHER RELATED TITLES

AN INTELLIGENT PERSON'S GUIDE TO EDUCATION

TONY LITTLE

BLOOMSBURY
LONDON · OXFORD · NEW YORK · NEW DELHI · SYDNEY

Bloomsbury Continuum

An imprint of Bloomsbury Publishing Plc

50 Bedford Square	1385 Broadway
London	New York
WC1B 3DP	NY 10018
UK	USA

www.bloomsbury.com

Bloomsbury, Continuum and the Diana logo are trademarks of Bloomsbury Publishing Plc

First published 2015

British Library Cataloguing-in-Publication Data
A catalogue record for this book is available from the British Library.

Library of Congress Cataloguing-in-Publication data has been applied for.

ISBN: HB:	978-1-4729-1311-1
ePDF:	978-1-4729-1313-5
ePub:	978-1-4729-1312-8

4 6 8 10 9 7 5 3

Typeset by Integra Software Services Pvt. Ltd.
Printed and bound in Great Britain by CPI Group (UK) Ltd, Croydon CR0 4YY

To find out more about our authors and books visit www.bloomsbury.com. Here you will find extracts, author interviews, details of forthcoming events and the option to sign up for our newsletters.

Jenny
without whom life as a headmaster would
have been impossible.

CONTENTS

CONTENTS

Introduction

The writing of this short book was prompted by parents. Whether the motivation was earnest enquiry or politeness, over the years parents of pupils in my schools have asked me to write down ideas they have heard me talk about either in private conversation or in a public forum. As I come to the end of my time as a head, reflection seems natural.

Whether or not they pay fees, parents invest a huge amount of themselves in their children's education. As a parent like any other, I know that a good education is the greatest gift we give our children and we want to do our best by them. Yet often parents feel at one remove, wary in a world at once familiar, yet strangely alien, like rereading a well-known story only to discover the text has changed. This book is for them.

What follows in these pages are thoughts and experiences from my life as a head. In essence, this book addresses three questions I have regularly been asked. What makes a good school? What have I learnt about teenagers along the way? What does a head actually *do*?

There is little reference in these pages to the great educational thinkers of our age and, I hope, even less use of jargon. This is, for the most part, homespun and personal, reflections from 26 years as a head of three rather different schools, including co-ed and single-sex, day and boarding.

Half of those years as a head have been spent at Eton College. Eton is a school which seems to exercise an unusual fascination in the public mind. Depending on your point of view, it is either a meritocratic centre of excellence or a symbol of values that should be destroyed in the pursuit of equality and social justice. I sometimes meet people who are unaware that Eton is a school with real live teenagers, who are much like teenagers everywhere.

There will be those who will say that the Head Master of Eton College has nothing worthwhile to say about education. They may well be right. Except that all teachers are part of our national conversation and should have something useful to say.

Inevitably what I think and write is strongly influenced by my experience, so teenage boys and boarding in the independent sector feature prominently in these pages, but part of the privilege of being at Eton is the passport it has given me to visit many schools at home and abroad, schools of apparently radically different style and context. Yet I have always felt at home. Whether in the East End of London or in a country prep school, whether in a tower-block in a Chinese city or a backwater village in Africa, a school is a school. There is a great deal more that brings parents and teachers together than separates.

Running as a kind of leitmotif in this book you will find references to A. C. Benson. Arthur Benson was a prolific writer, intimately connected with the worlds of literature, the church and academe in the high Victorian period. He was also a schoolmaster at Eton. In 1902 he published a short book describing and commentating upon his chosen profession. I find *The Schoolmaster* an extraordinary read, part window on assumptions and ideas now out of fashion, part repository of enduring wisdom. At the least, reference to his observations more than one hundred years ago serves to highlight attitudes in our own time.

The issues, problems and joys of education are universal.

1

'What Good are Schools?'

It was a hazy, heady afternoon and I was bored. I was a trainee teacher trundling through a succession of courses of variable quality and facing the prospect of a session with a less than stimulating title, something along the lines of 'Evaluations of school systems'. The speaker was introduced. His appearance was arresting: a pale face, a penetrating eye and a wizened arm. His opening words were more arresting still: 'Schools are evil and you who are about to teach in schools will participate in evil.'

As a young trainee teacher I was used to having to fend off barbs from friends, along the lines that teaching was a dead-end job with no prospects, suitable only for people who could not really do anything else. But to be described as the spawn of the devil was something of a new departure. Our speaker turned out to be a disciple of Ivan Illich, of whom more later, and for the first time he gave me cause to think properly about the institutions we call schools. It is a ready enough assumption to accept what is familiar, but actually, I thought, what good are these places we call schools?

There is a distinct strand in English literature which takes issue with the whole business of schooling, along the lines of Saki: 'Good gracious, you have to educate him first. You can't expect a boy to be vicious until he has been to a good school.' This kind of approach is summed up in Osbert Sitwell's memorable description of his education in *Who's Who*, 'Educ: during the holidays from Eton'. It may be that writers such as these entertain some deep underlying belief that schools cause actual harm, but I doubt it; rather, these are the satirical flourishes of people who have the privilege of a good education and come from educated families. Being dismissive of something that has come easily to you is a common enough human trait.

By contrast, political and social visionaries tend to see education as the answer to everything. With the full force of Fabian rhetoric H.G. Wells said that 'human history becomes more and more a race between education and catastrophe'. The idea that education is central to the health and development of national public life has become a distinct strand of mainstream politics, whether it is Tony Blair's raising of the banner 'education, education, education' in 1997 as the focus for his premiership, or the heroic rhythms of Michael Gove as Secretary of State, 'We must be uncompromising in our vigilance, we must be unyielding in our resolve. Sweeping reform is spurred by moral imperative ... '

It is worth peeling away the rhetoric and satire to pin down what we mean by education. At the risk of being a schoolmaster pedant, it is instructive to look at the etymological root of the word. There appears to be a choice of two familiar-sounding Latin words: *educare* and *educere*. *Educere* means to lead forth troops, preparing them for battle, which brings with it a resonance of drill. *Educare* means to nurture, to bring up, to tend and support for growth. The latter is the correct derivation but it is interesting that these two ideas have been confused over the centuries. Even today a typical dictionary definition describes 'education' as imparting 'knowledge by formal instruction to a pupil'. In my own mind I have an image based on the archaic English verb 'to educe', meaning 'to lead forth as a river'. The idea that we learn by finding our own way as a river does down to the sea, rather than being channelled and directed, is a powerful one. This is expressed well by Muriel Spark through the words of her eponymous character Miss Jean Brodie, who criticises her colleague Miss Mackay for, 'putting in something that is not there and that is not what I call education, I call it intrusion.'

The two descriptions of education prompted by the *educare/educere* debate neatly frame the central juxtaposition. Is the education we wish for our young people to be delivered through formal instruction by imparting particular knowledge and developing certain skills, or is it the nurturing of an individual's natural abilities to their limits?

Most of us would say that the education we want for our children is a balance between the two, but as we glance around the world this is not self-evident. In China, for example, a combination of culture (a Confucian belief in the teacher as sage to whom pupils must and will listen) and logistics (with, typically, 50 students in a classroom) has led to a deep-rooted belief in the power of instruction.

Whichever view one takes there is still an underlying assumption that there is innate worth in an institution that brings young people together in one place for their education. Why should this be so?

Let us return to the man with the withered arm. Quoting from Ivan Illich's *De-schooling Society* published in 1971, he told his audience of teacher students, 'the escalation of the school is as destructive as the escalation of weapons but less visibly so'. That schools are weapons of mass destruction is a robust claim and, as a consequence, perhaps easy to reject. Illich does, however, make some telling points. Whether they are good or bad, Illich would claim that schools of their very nature are divisive because the unit of the school will reflect divisions of class, religion and culture, and setting these randomly constructed units against each other (for example in a league table) is an absurdity. Schools are also oppressive because they restrict natural desires, ambitions and feelings; they are anti-individual and, in effect, exercises in mass control. In any event, Illich would say, there is something rather patronizing about young people of a certain age being corralled into institutions where they are told what to do and what to think. Schools are mechanistic; their structure of classes, routines and timetabling takes away freedom of development. They offer a paradigm of capitalist society. And the list goes on. In essence, the argument runs, schools are counter-productive: claims that schools produce rounded individuals are bogus; instead, they produce stunted, lop-sided people who are fodder for the machine of society.

Illich has a view of society in which education is available to the individual whenever he or she wants it. If a 40-year-old feels the need to take a maths course, then that is when it should be taken. The barriers of adolescence and school leaving age would no longer apply – no more would education 'be wasted on the young'. It is hard not to be strongly attracted by this ideal of a life of constant self-development. I share his concern that the nation state tends to engage in top-down control of schools and I share his hope that each individual has the capacity to develop unique attitudes and skills. Indeed, I passionately believe that we have the capacity to shape our own destinies. Where I part company with this optimistic view of society is in the belief that human beings really will seek out education at some stage when they feel like it. This is where schools come in.

At its simplest schools give young people a place at the water's edge. A horse may not choose to drink if it is led to water but it cannot drink at all if the water is not there.

Schools are an efficient way to train young people in ways that have come to be seen as essential by society. While encouraging young people to think for themselves is the key to any good education, received wisdom is a useful guide to learning how to use the tools. With the tools in hand, you can learn how to learn.

Schools are also relatively cost-effective ways to help young people engage with the skills and attitudes that will help them navigate adult life. Unromantic as it sounds, one of the great benefits of negotiating the rhythms of school life is the opposite of the 'mechanistic' criticism. Schools are indeed built around routines of one kind or another, and understanding the value of routines, how they can create time and liberate the individual, is a great lesson for a teenager to learn.

But where schools really come into their own is as communities allowing young people to develop an understanding of diverse relationships, offering them role models outside the home and helping to inculcate the standards and values necessary for social living; in short, learning to be part of the tribe. Crucially, this preparation for the tribe includes learning where the parameters of behaviour lie, learning to accept and value discipline. Society needs individuality, imagination and energy to drive forwards, but just as importantly it needs individuals to exercise restraint. Curbing personal dreams for a greater good is a defining mark of civilization. Schools should be the medium to achieve both aims: schools make sense.

The point of schools: a test for teenagers

When encouraging teenage students to reflect on the point and purpose of their education, I have used the following text taken from Benjamin Franklin's *Remarks concerning the Savages of North America*:

At the treaty of Lancaster in Pennsylvania, anno 1744, between the government of Virginia and the Six Nations, the commissioners from Virginia acquainted the Indians by a speech, that there was at Williamsburg a College with a fund for educating Indian youth; and if the chiefs of the six Nations would send down half a dozen of their sons to that college, the government would take care that they be well provided for, and instructed in all the learning of the White People. The Indians' spokesman replied: We know that you highly esteem the kind of learning taught in those colleges, and that the maintenance of our young men, while with you, would be very expensive to you. We are convinced, therefore, that you mean to do us good by your proposal and we thank you heartily.

But you who are wise, must know that different nations have different conceptions of things; and you will not therefore take it amiss, if our ideas of this kind of education happen not to be the same with yours. We have some experience of it; several of our young people were formerly brought up at the colleges of the

Northern Provinces; they were instructed in all your sciences; but, when they came back to us, they were bad runners, ignorant of every means of living in the woods, unable to bear either cold or hunger, knew neither how to build a cabin, take a deer, nor kill an enemy, spoke our language imperfectly, were therefore neither fit for hunters, warriors nor counsellors; they were totally good for nothing.

We are however not the less obligated by your kind offer, though we decline accepting it, and to show our grateful sense of it, if the gentlemen of Virginia will send us a dozen of their sons; we will take care of their education, instruct them in all we know, and make men of them.

The value to us of our schools in large measure is determined by our views and prejudices, often deep-rooted. I give my students a set of questions taken from an old International Baccalaureate task and ask them to consider a response from the Native Americans of Benjamin Franklin's account.

- *What are the aims of the school of which you are a part? What through the aims are you expected to know?* In the case of the native Americans an answer might be to become an outstanding huntsman in all weathers.

- *What are the ideals of the school that have determined those aims?* Perhaps a belief in oneness with nature.

- *Where did those ideals come from? On what grounds are they justified?* The ideals might be beyond memory, inherited traditions through stories and song and justified by the cycle of life, as day follows night and death follows life.

- *What conflicts can arise from these ideas?* In an established natural order it may be difficult to make sense of abnormality, an eclipse of the sun, earthquake or the coming of the white man.

This provides an enjoyable exercise, prompting a great deal of discussion usually characterized by students' sense of high moral purpose about education coupled with scepticism about adult role models in the public eye. They tend to be light on history (where our ideals have come from) and long on debates about conflict. But it makes them think.

Reflecting on personal and communal experience and analysing the purpose of education are essential ways for students to come to a better understanding of themselves and their connection to society.

In Britain, sadly, there is no obligation for schools to engage their students in this process. Good schools do so intuitively.

2

The Shrinking Curriculum

In place of educational vision, we tinker with the system. This is a sorry truth about British education.

Between the Butler Act of 1944 – which heralded grammar, technical and secondary modern schools – and the introduction of the National Curriculum in 1988, there was relatively little legislation in education, notwithstanding the introduction of comprehensive schools. Since 1988 there has been almost one major piece of legislation each year. Each new act has represented the temporary victory of a point of view, not a national consensus. There has been a loss of confidence and shared belief in the function and purpose of schools. For example, should funding of state schools be centralized or local? Are issues of admissions or exclusions to do with the rights of the individual or the common good? More importantly, should the emphasis of school education be to produce effective competitors in a global market place or free-thinkers with a rich spiritual life? Is education a means to an end or a thing in itself?

In a characteristically British way, over the centuries there has been a largely unwritten consensus about the fundamental values and underlying aims of schooling which, broadly speaking, might be described as the development of character, conscience and clean living, with intellectual precision for those who could cope with it. In more recent times this consensus has been more difficult to achieve as fixed points in our social landscape have shifted or disappeared.

In place of consensus, successive generations of politicians have retreated behind a wall of statistics. Their shared message seems to be: if in doubt, measure the things that can be measured, ignore those that cannot, but demonstrate to the public that the statistics show education is clearly improving. It is a sad thing: where once men spoke of the Age of Enlightenment, we now live in the great Age of Measurement.

Yet this is not one lingering, dark cloud of gloom. A great deal has happened in my professional lifetime to make schools better places: inspection regimes, for example, although time-consuming and irritating at the time, help focus our minds on the way we run our schools. I have not the slightest doubt that most schools today react more swiftly and sensitively in matters of child protection, for example, than ever was the case 20 years ago. So, too, league tables, misleading though they can be and misinterpreted though they frequently are. Some shadowy self-delusions have been blown away and this can only be a good thing. I remember the shock of some former pupils when I was headmaster of Chigwell School, at that time a decent, averagely performing school, when the first tables revealed that their school was not one of the national top three, as they had happily imagined. It is hard for puffed-up parochialism to survive the brisk wind of comparison with a wider world.

There is a good case for rigorous assessment. By analysing regular measurements of children's performance, a sharp light can be shone on specific areas where improvement should be made. It is, the proponents argue, a clean and effective way to raise standards. By shining an even bigger light on the performance of the school as a whole, pressure is maintained on the professionals to do right by the children. This is a logical approach and, up to a point, it works. There is no doubt that basic competence in some areas of the curriculum has improved. But it comes at a cost.

A great deal depends on what is chosen to be measured and how it is done. If the prescribed literary text is safe and 'accessible' (sometimes a euphemism for 'undemanding'), or if history is only a routine diet of Nazism with a splash of Tudors, or if a subject is broken into disparate segments, we are not measuring the capacity of our young people to see to the horizon.

The very business of measurement should carry a health warning. It should be obligatory for teenagers to be shown how the same statistics can produce a completely different rank order depending on the method used; how statistics can be used to prop up an argument or a cause. Adults need reminding, too. As a professional well versed in the capacity of statistics to mislead, I still find my eye drawn to a league table position. And mislead they certainly do. A comparative table can be distorted by changing the rubric; so, for example, the international version of GCSE is excluded from tables, as a consequence of which some of the top-performing schools in the country are rated as scoring 0 per cent.

The problem with statistical tables is not so much their utility as the undue significance placed upon them. They offer a helpful guide to some aspects of performance, but they do not come close to revealing the full picture. A school appears to hover around the top of an A Level table, but what does the table tell you about the school's admissions process or the hurdles it places in front of its pupils even to enter the sixth form? League tables say as much about intake as outcome.

It is understood that raw statistics can mislead, so various 'value added' measures have been introduced, but many parents find them hard to fathom. In order to appreciate the context of each child's performance, a matrix of information is needed, and even then it is easy to pick holes in the method. It is a convoluted business and it is understandable that a simple record of exam results, presented in football league fashion, attracts the most interest.

The pressure on schools from league tables should not be underestimated, however. Small shifts of percentage point can loom large in teachers' minds. It does not take much of a downward change in a year's results for the school to be described as 'plummeting' in the local press, with an adverse effect on admissions. In this climate it can be no surprise that schools sometimes adapt the programme they offer children. Some schools have identified easier subjects or exam routes that offer multiple GCSE grades for one subject. At primary level, fear of published tables has led some schools to concentrate mainly on maths and 'literacy' for SATS tests, with all the work in history, geography and science for the year recorded in the same, slender exercise book. It has led to a narrowing of experience for children; the curriculum has shrunk.

This narrowing of focus has also been seen in subject syllabuses. A low point some years ago was reducing the content of the science syllabus at GCSE and expressing scientific concepts in the form of stories, thereby 'contextualizing' scientific understanding. The effect of this was to rip out a sense of the grammar and the vocabulary of science. Just as with languages, so too there is a grammar and a vocabulary to be learnt in science or mathematics or the humanities. There are no short cuts to intellectual development, and the academic attainment that comes with it comes from hard work, from addressing matters one initially does not understand, from perseverance and commitment.

The real problem with measurement culture, however, has been the increasing dependency of the pupil on the teacher. This is clear to see. Exam grades are promoted as the most significant part of a child's schooling, so it should be no surprise that pupils and teachers, both concerned about the next step on the measurement ladder, focus squarely on the exam syllabus to the detriment of almost anything else. Yet common sense, as well as current research in the learning sciences, suggests that the ultimate success of a school career is when pupils are weaned off instruction and can work things out for themselves.

We have more public examinations for teenagers than anywhere else in Western Europe. Over the past 20 years British teachers have become ever more efficient at enabling school pupils to jump through very specific, rather narrow hoops. The scope for creative inspiration and divergent thinking is now extremely limited. A while ago an outstanding sixth-form historian at Eton was bemused to discover that one of his six otherwise top-scoring modules at A Level had been graded U – off the scale, a bad fail. We discovered that he had seen a flaw in the setting of a question and turned it inside out in an essay deemed 'brilliant' and 'degree-level' by two Oxbridge dons, but his answer did not fit the template of the mark scheme and the unclassified grade stood. There was a price to pay: the boy dropped a grade at A Level and lost his university place.

He was a victim of the atomizing of education that has characterized the last couple of decades. With a diminishing belief in an overarching purpose we have tended to identify the constituent parts of the curriculum that can be held up to the light and assessed.

In so doing, we have created a straitjacket. The message we have given our children is that assessments and exams are no longer milestones on a journey, but the sole purpose and destination. Routinely I hear children in school use the word 'education' to mean exams, as in, 'I don't want music/sport/social service to get in the way of my education.' We have impoverished our own children.

The recently announced move towards two-year A Level courses offers a welcome reduction in the volume of examining. However, it remains the case that teenagers apply to university and are offered places before the results of their A Levels, Pre-U or IB are even known. The pressure becomes intense. Aspirational sixteen-year-olds know that they must achieve a raft of top grades at GCSE even to be considered for competitive courses. To a degree unimaginable a generation ago, we have decided to prejudice the chances of late developers, those pupils who sit on indifferent GCSE grades, but who come alive in the sixth form. Some universities freely admit that they value GCSE grades achieved by 16-year-olds as a more reliable indicator of future performance than A Levels. What a crazy system!

A lack of trust in the teaching profession has led to a desire to control and direct the affairs of schools from the outside. To me, this smacks of desperation. Our system is inside out. As we will see in the next chapter, the most successful European national system of education invests in teacher training of high quality sustained throughout a teacher's career. This breeds confidence, the confidence to allow teachers freedom to teach. In the UK, teacher training is in a mess. Rather than sort it out, we have relied on top-down control and measurement by results.

There have been some significant steps forward to allow some greater autonomy in schools through the Academies programme and greater diversity through the Free School initiative, but no structural realignment will compensate for really effective teacher training. While I welcome greater diversity in schools, and while there are some notable individual success stories, they can only be truly of value in a culture in which there is an underlying agreement about the purpose of schools generally. In such a culture, a diverse mix of schools will highlight different paths to the same broad goals. In the absence of that consensus, they will at best be pinpricks of light and will not illuminate the nation.

It is understandable that heads often feel on the back foot, beset not only by ever-growing administrative burdens and reduced time to get everything done, but also by changing expectations from parents. I have enjoyed my relationship with many parents, sensing that we see ourselves on the same side, but I have to admit that some underlying assumptions have changed. Supermarket choice is a feature of the modern age and seems now accepted as a necessary virtue. The customer has the right to expect and demand particular, personalized services, has a right to complain if this service is not delivered to his satisfaction, and has the right to expect compensation when disappointed. If you believe, as I do, in personal freedom and choice, applying this philosophy to schooling seems to make sense. I have certainly heard business-minded school governors speak glowingly of the power of the customer and choice.

Yet there is danger here. I also believe in personal responsibility, commitment and duty. Heads and teachers deal, of course, not with commodities but with young people who are forming for themselves their perceptions of the world. They need guidance, they need to understand that consequences follow actions, that difference enriches life, that individuals have responsibilities as well as rights. While they may pay lip service to these aims, by no means do all parents subscribe to them, nor, indeed, exemplify them. It is harder to stand for values in which you believe and which you see as interweaving strands that form a complete and strong totality, when some parents pick and choose – and sometimes pick and mix. The father aggressively urging victory at all costs on the touchline, the mother bullying staff to change teaching arrangements, the parents wholly supportive of the school's disciplinary policy until it affects their child – such parents hinder and even damage their children. Schools should always seek the active, purposeful support of parents, which is frequently given. They should always seek to explain to parents why a particular action is right, and this is frequently understood. But teachers also know that parents are sometimes wrong, even about their own children, and while some of them may see themselves solely as customers in the relationship, teachers have a duty as experienced, professional people to stand up for the school, its values and the child.

How do we change things?

There is no template solution. Indeed, one of the problems we have faced in recent times has been the tendency for pundits and politicians to talk as though it is possible to make sense of education largely in structural terms. The way we learn and connect is nuanced, multi-layered, organic: pouring this expertise into a mould produces a rigid shape, the antithesis of a developing, dynamic lifetime of engagement with new ideas. I want to break a mould, but I am not a vandal – there is need for shape in the way we educate our young but it must be responsive and flexible.

The key is focusing on the individual child, an idea that has a deep resonance in Western culture, an idea invigorated in Christian thought. We hear in the Gospels that Jesus came alongside man. Good teachers come alongside their pupils. This hugely important idea may resonate across the centuries but we have done our best to drown out its call in a bustle of initiatives, restructuring and systems of accountability.

Yet this focus on the individual child, important though it is, only makes sense if we revitalize the idea that education is a social, communal activity. In a sense, we have come to place too much weight on the significance of schools. Education is at its most vital and effective when there is coordination between family, school and community. Families should not abrogate their responsibility for the education of their children solely to an institution called 'school'. Similarly, involvement by the broader community in schools through local businesses, civic groups and charitable organizations, for example, and of the school in the broader community, not only increases opportunities for young people but helps them put what they do in school into context. School becomes part of the warp and weft of living, not a separate experience, cut off from real life.

A good number of schools seek to connect their pupils with the wider world, but the pressure of measurement culture militates against placing this activity at the heart of school life. To move from a cult of individual performance to a more community-minded understanding would take a cultural shift of considerable proportions. It would be too easy to characterize the difference as a straight choice between sharp-elbowed go-getters on the one hand and soft-hearted consensus-seekers on the other. In order to compete with the world's best our young people will need to be adaptable and independent-minded, based on the secure foundation of well-established skills and knowledge; but they will also need to be creative thinkers and doers; and, for all our sakes, we need them to be socially aware, compassionate, community-builders, too. At present our approach is lopsided.

Redressing the balance

We are some way from realizing a vision where the ideal of education is to excite and inspire young people towards their lifelong self-development. Pupil and teacher are too caught up in scrabbling for exam grades to have the luxury of a view to the horizon. There are, however, some steps we can take in the short term to redress the balance. We can insist that university places are offered only on the basis of known achievement by students at the age of 18. If the universities wish to rework A Levels or the academic requirements for entry, that is fine. Indeed, universities should be expected to take a lead in shaping and giving texture to the way we assess 18-year-olds so that there is effective continuity between school and higher education, thus avoiding the stop and go that characterizes our current arrangements. But no university place should be awarded on the basis of what a student achieves *before* the age of 18.

So let's scrap the GCSE altogether: what purpose does it serve? The nation requires a snapshot of performance in key skills at the point of the legal school-leaving age, so let us have a basic matriculation requirement in English, Maths, Science and maybe a modern language: no more than this. Then we can liberate schools and teachers inventively to devise, teach and assess courses beyond the confines of current exam syllabuses. Outside the group of matriculation subjects, we should come alongside young people and play to their enthusiasms and strengths. These courses could be externally moderated so that young people leaving school at 16 would have a portfolio of assessed skills and demonstrable achievement in things that matter to them. Academically inspired students could push ahead, avoiding the painful experience described by one Head of Department who strongly felt that pupils have to unlearn the habits that win a top grade at GCSE in order to become good A–level candidates. Aspirant engineers, for example, could be given a collaborative experience of practical engineering far beyond what is possible with current constraints. Remove the GCSE as it currently stands and we unblock a logjam.

But we need to go a step further. The academic curriculum gains its integrity by being an integral but integrated part of the whole curriculum. Physical activity, team games, artistic creativity, spiritual richness and emotional maturity are all partners in the successful growth of our young people. Through the nineteenth century and into the twentieth, public opinion accepted this wholeness of approach to the education of our young as a vital truth. Now not so. Indeed, it is a measure of the extent to which our focus has shifted, how dominated our thinking has become by measurable success in academic terms, that there has been felt to be the need to bolt on programmes that meet perceived failings – leadership one year, citizenship the next and so on – and I would include happiness lessons in this group. We should not need this segmented approach, which can only offer a stop-gap shoring up of the building from the outside. The British tradition of holistic, liberal education has been one of the glories of our development as a society – and we must reclaim it.

One way to reclaim the holistic tradition is to place it at the centre of inspection. A school might be deemed satisfactory based on the measurable achievement of its pupils; indeed, it is essential that a school's basic competence is assessed clearly according to measurable criteria; but to be rated good or outstanding should require a different level of effectiveness and aspiration, embracing not only the curriculum as a whole, but also the vital, intangible aspects that make a school vibrant: its relationships, dynamism and ethos. These require judgements to be made without the crutch of statistics, by inspectors with the knowledge, vision and permission to come out from behind a barrier of formulae and templates.

It would be good, too, if they were enabled to use language that reflects life, rather than officialese. I recall an inspection judgement at one school that referred to the 'tyranny of the school bus', a phrase that exactly captured a major problem for the school (that the after-school, extra-curricular programme did not happen) but which was deemed an inappropriate phrase and removed from the report.

Although it is a mighty challenge for any inspection regime to report confidently on matters not rooted in hard facts, and while there would be a minefield of problems to negotiate, we must find a voice for holistic education and let it sing.

One of the ironies of the situation is that educators overseas view this British tradition as something to be strived for, or at least interpreted into another culture in order to release its benefits. The top-performing OECD area in PISA assessments, under most headings, is Shanghai. Yet it was in Shanghai, in conversation with heads of the leading schools in the area, that head teachers' concern and frustration about the failings of Chinese education became apparent to me. They know their students produce unsurpassed results in examined conditions in what they describe as 'theoretical education' but the system that seems to serve Chinese students so well does not help them develop a range of skills that the Chinese themselves increasingly perceive are essential for a globalized economy: practical application of knowledge, the ability to present clearly and well, flexible thinking and so on. They feel trapped by the restrictions of the Gaocow, the end-of-school national assessment, the equivalent of A Levels. Does this sound familiar? As one of the most distinguished heads in Shanghai put it to me: 'We know we are on a juggernaut heading for the cliff edge, and we want to change direction, but we don't know how.'

You may think this reaction demonstrates the innate propensity of schoolteachers to find gloom wherever they may be: not so. The Chinese reaction illustrates the vitality and value of the liberal British holistic tradition – high-performing Chinese schools are fascinated by the philosophy and methodology of the best British schools. Let us take stock: this is an extraordinary thing. China, the new superpower that will soon be the largest English-speaking nation in the world and which has more gifted and talented students than we have students altogether, sees more in a British style of education than we seem to value.

Maybe there is another reason for the Chinese interest. In PISA assessments Shanghai may be at the top, with the UK seeming to be heading for the relegation zone on most measurements, but there is another group that matches the Shanghai schools: the UK independent sector. That there should be such a gulf of achievement between state and independent schools in the same country is a matter of national shame. Bearing in mind that many UK independent schools are not selective, the gap is the more striking. I would argue that one key reason behind this disparity is the continuing commitment to an all-round education, with strong support of the individual, that is whole-heartedly embraced by most good independent schools.

As a nation, we will only recapture a traditional strength, and give our young people the confidence to face change and uncertainty, if we loosen the grip of measurement-driven schooling and at the same time assert the demonstrable benefit of a school culture that celebrates academic excellence and the acquisition of skills, but which is firmly grounded in, and shaped by, personal relationships.

What really matters in a school, when you take away the structures and systems and rules that give a necessary shape to communal lives, are the people and the quality of their relationships. I want young men to leave my school who are confident and independent-minded. I want them to feel that they are unique individuals. But the unfettered exercise of individualism is a curse. Edmund Burke knew it when he watched the unfolding of the French Revolution in 1790 and wrote in words that seem remarkably relevant to us today: any society that destroys the fabric of its state must soon be 'disconnected into the dust and powder of individuality'.

I want my young men to understand that simple but startling truth that we are unique individuals, but we are part of other people, too, shaped and tuned by those around us. I want them to understand how it is that aggressive self-assertion leads to 'dust and powder'. I want them to know that nothing is permanent and that we create our communities day by day or they die.

How relationships develop between young people and, just as importantly, between young people and adults should be right at the centre of our school programmes, the starting point for all our discussions about syllabuses and systems.

Short-termism prevails. I have been to meetings of head teachers from a mixed bag of schools, state and independent, at which the only topics occupying them were those assumed directly to lead to exam-grade improvement. The only discussion worth having, it seemed, was how to shoehorn additional teaching, through master classes, into the teaching day or how to use new data systems forensically to identify students' exam weaknesses in order to bump them up a grade.

Yet I have also seen good, practical examples where schools have recognized the power of working through relationships: in one London comprehensive school, a commitment to vertical tutor groups, an idea borrowed from the traditional boarding house model, in which older teenagers take direct responsibility for younger pupils; in another, a comprehensive school head asking for trained volunteer sixth-form mentors from an academically selective neighbouring school, in order to form a relationship and work alongside GCSE students, with dramatically improved results; in a Midlands comprehensive, encouraging pupils to engage positively with the management of the school, including, for example, school pupils trained to observe and report on the quality of teaching; in another school, pupils taking the responsibility to ask the teacher of their choice to be their personal tutor. Relationships in school work when all those involved know that they are taken seriously.

We must pay proper attention, too, to the relationships *between* schools. In so doing, incidentally, we would respond to one of Illich's criticisms that schools are created as competitive units and encourage a dislocated view of society. There is a great deal to applaud in moves to give those who work in state-maintained schools more autonomy, but not at the expense of collaboration. Pupils and teachers directly benefit from exposure to the culture of other schools.

I have witnessed the revelation that comes from such collaboration time and again: students from two schools of apparently similar academic standing discovering different emphases and approaches to a problem or a text; students from very different schools encountering the human truth behind social masks; teachers seeing different contexts at work, which gives them the confidence to deal with the very high-achieving student or the child with a marked learning difficulty.

The antidote to the shrinking curriculum is to be found in celebrating holistic education, in relationships, in creating flexible routes for pupils – and in trust.

We have a habit of complicating the business of educating young people; we seem to have been adept at creating a maze where a path is needed. As technological advances introduce change at an ever-faster rate, we run the risk of creating an ever more intricate maze. Yet, in essence, it increasingly seems to me that at heart education is a simple thing and we need to hold fast to this simplicity. It comes down to two words. I know the phrase I am about to use may sound like some wacky social movement from the 1920s, but I will chance the words anyway: joy and love. Education is about the joy of learning, of discovery, of achievement, your own and other people's; and about love of fellow man. Everything else is just a means to an end.

3

Vocation, Vocation, Vocation

In 2005 workmen renovating a room in the corner of the medieval cloisters of Eton College uncovered some faint images under wood panelling. They had discovered fragments of a wall painting which required some close scrutiny and imagination to piece the picture together. The painting is of a classroom scene dated around 1520 and is believed to be the earliest representation of a school scene in England. To the right is a group of boys sitting on their form, some assiduously working, some idling, some mucking about. To the far right is the shape of a boy with his arm raised but, I was relieved to discover, not attempting to knock seven bells out of another boy, but in the act of striking his hoop. He is at the far side of the picture away from the authoritarian (and physically enormous) figure of the Master who holds centre stage, but above his head is the Latin tag *incipe parve puer*, which loosely translated would read 'get a grip little boy'. The painting has a sprinkling of observations and comments. It is a vignette of life in the schoolroom as it was lived every day, designed for public display in what was, in effect, the front office. On one level this is advertising, the first school prospectus.

At the top of the wall crowning this schoolroom scene is a banner headline – the strapline of modern marketing. It is a quotation from Quintilian: *Virtuo preceptoris est ingeniorum notare discrimina*, which means 'the excellence of the teacher is to identify the differences in talents of pupils'. When I saw it I was amazed. Here in the early days of Eton College was a statement of belief in the purpose of good teaching, taken from a source almost two thousand years old, which has held true through the ages. From time to time someone invents a new piece of jargon as if creating a new vision, but usually this is merely reviving an old idea. For example, the jargon word 'differentiation', much in use over the past twenty years, broadly speaking means identifying the different talents of pupils in order to help them achieve their potential. This is not a complex proposition, though sometimes challenging to enact, yet we lose sight of it under a welter of complications, like hiding a painting under wood panelling. We would do well to hold up the beliefs and practice of the past to the light. We may well find illumination.

One clear lesson from history is the central significance of good teachers in the development of our children. Yet in Britain we have sustained an ambivalent attitude to teachers. To some people the dictum, 'those who can, do; those who can't, teach' is not just a throwaway line. The ideal of the teacher/sage has vibrant resonances in diverse cultures from ancient Greece to Japan, yet it finds only a faint echo in the Anglo-Saxon world. On the other hand, parents' experience of individual teachers is usually very positive and public polls about the relative value of professions tend to show teaching in a very good light, some way above lawyers and politicians. In the public arena, the British have a habit of arguing about potential structures and systems of governance, about accountability and outcomes, rather than focusing on the quality of teachers and their teaching.

There is a lack of trust in schools and teachers. There are some good reasons for this: too many poorly trained, inadequate teachers have survived in the system for too long, and there has not been a coherent attempt by teachers themselves to express clearly what they believe is the purpose of what they are doing. However, it is also the case that schools and their teachers have been increasingly asked to shoulder the burdens of social problems that should be the shared responsibility of others in society, especially the family.

Behind thoughts about the culture, curriculum and the purpose of schools lies one radical idea, an idea both simple and profound, easy to express, harder to embed. We must learn to trust the teacher. Right now teaching is the bastard profession. As parents, we expect our children's teachers to have professional competence and, indeed, rather higher personal standards than society at large. Yet we have all been to school, so we all know about teachers and teaching. We know our children better than the teacher and, frankly, could tell the teacher a thing or two about his business.

A. C. Benson did not think much of teacher training. It was, he said 'like training people to become good conversationalists'. All that is needed are subject knowledge and 'a lively, genial and effective personality'. The qualities he lists are much to be desired, but the thrust of his argument was wrong then and it is certainly wrong now.

Teachers should be excellently trained professionals and, as a consequence, earn respect. Trust is born from more than professional training; it stems from a parent or a child's belief that the teacher cares, really cares. And this is the sadness of it. I come across many teachers in many different types of school in the UK who actively do really care, but they feel they are not properly professionally trained, supported or respected.

This is not the case in other European countries. The poster boys and girls of effective modern Western education are the Finns. Repeated international measurements show the Finns in the top handful of nations: Finland seems to have got it right. The story of Finland's development is both impressive and instructive. Faced with calamity during the Second World War, they were obliged to think from scratch about their society and how to sustain and enrich it through education. As a relatively small and homogeneous society, the Finns have not had to face the particular challenges of a large, multi-cultural country, but their challenges were sharp and real. And the secret at the heart of their success?

Pasi Sahlberg, former Director General at the Centre for International Mobility and Co-operation in the Finnish Ministry of Education, writes:

> Many factors have contributed to Finland's educational system's current fame, such as its 9 year comprehensive school for all children, modern learning-focused curricula, systematic care for students with diverse special needs, and local autonomy and shared responsibility. However, research and experience suggest that one factor trumps all others: the daily contribution of excellent teachers.

School teaching in Finland is a prestigious and socially desirable career. A virtuous circle has been created so that Finland is possibly the only nation able to recruit its primary school teachers from the top quintile of all 18-year-old school leavers. Sahlberg identifies competition for places on teacher training courses as one significant benefit (competition breeds competition: in 2010 there were some 6,600 new applicants for 660 available places on the primary school teacher education programme at Finnish universities). Salaries are close to the national average and offer no particular incentive, though the salary ladder rewards experience more in Finland than in other countries. Of paramount importance, however, is that the teachers' workplaces allow them to 'fulfil their moral missions'. In the Finnish system, teachers expect to be given the full range of professional autonomy to practise what they have been educated to do. Teachers in Finland are enabled to feel that they have professional esteem on a par with lawyers, doctors and engineers.

The foundation for this confidence and shared sense of moral purpose comes though the way would-be teachers are selected and educated. All teachers must follow a thorough university degree course to Masters level taking some 5–7 years to complete: teacher education is recognized as a mainstream and important element of university life. There is a clear direction here: there are no short cuts, no alternative ways into the profession.

By contrast, Britain has been in a muddle for years. For a start there has been an assumption that new teachers need to be trained, not educated. This is more than semantics. Degrees in education have been rather looked down on: the preferred route has been a degree in a specialist academic subject with a bolt-on course of training. The one-year Post Graduate Certificate in Education that I took in the mid-1970s was, mostly, a waste of time. There were teaching practices that offered valuable dedicated time in which to experiment and make mistakes and there were some useful conversations along the way, but the philosophical underpinning was slight and the lack of professionalism of some of the staff was laughable. It was perhaps the nature of the time to have one-dimensional Marxists trotting out their mantras, but it was the sloppiness that riled the teacher-student. One course in Professional Preparation was marked by the slovenliness of the tutor, who was always late and clearly uninterested. In retrospect, I suspect we learnt quite a lot from him.

The situation has not improved much over the past 40 years. Indeed, we seem to have had a collective loss of heart as the teacher training courses that exist begin to wither away: more universities are querying the viability of the courses they run. There is a deliberate switch of emphasis away from universities towards school-based programmes which would offer, in effect, 'on the job' training. As university training courses fall away, however, there is no established, functioning alternative. All the indications are that we will face a major shortfall of well-qualified teachers, a consequence mainly of muddled thinking and the lack of a coherent plan. The supply chain has been broken: it looks like vandalism.

As a head teacher my most significant act is the appointment of the best teachers I can find. I am in a dilemma: I value the well-grounded, thorough, continuing education of teachers, but I increasingly employ talented people with no teacher training qualification at all. In recent years I have engaged a raft of people – solicitor, army officer, trader on the financial markets, barrister and literary editor as well as young, untried graduates. They are intelligent, well-motivated people who have responded well to the ethos of the school and the support they are given. On-the-job training works pretty well in terms of basic practice, but it is not enough to build the level of highly effective professionalism found in Finland. Nor can we plug the gaps with schemes like TeachFirst, inventive and effective though it has been in the short term.

If we are to be serious about the progress of our education of school-aged children, we must demand an all-graduate entry with sustained education of our teachers throughout their careers and with salary levels reflecting the degree of teachers' experience of teaching and their own learning. I would rather have open house in the employment of new teachers for a trial period, two to three years, so that they can gain a proper sense of the joys and tribulations of teaching before committing themselves to career-long personal development leading to recognition as a qualified professional, the equivalent of the charter mark in other professions. Successful businesses know that in order to sustain their success they need to invest in the skills of their workforce. Teaching is our most important national business and we dabble.

One further reference to the Finns. It can be rather irritating to have someone else's work held up as the answer, and in truth there are no panaceas: the Finns are aware of the problems and challenges they face. Yet there is one other area in which they lead the way: research.

The same successful business that invests in the skills of the workplace is serious about research and development. So are the Finns. The obligation that teachers should hold academic Masters' degrees has elevated teachers as professionals who understand teaching holistically and improve their own work continuously. Teachers are expected to have a deep knowledge of the most recent advances in their subjects and in the practice of teaching; they are expected to embrace a research-based approach to their own work, regularly analysing what they do and being open-minded to change; and they are expected to see teacher education itself as the object of study and research. Professor Hansele Nierin of the University of Helsinki sees research-based teacher education as essential in creating the 'moral purpose and independent professional ethos' that leads to widespread trust.

Since the turn of the century, increasing numbers of British schools have shone a sharper light on what actually goes on in the classroom. The senior post of 'Head of Teaching and Learning' is now customary. This marks a welcome step forward from a traditional assumption that osmosis is the only true way for a teacher to learn his craft. In a rather smaller number of cases, this focus has led schools to see the value of research. More than anything, the habit of research bespeaks a frame of mind. Eton has opened a Centre of Innovation and Research in Learning to bring together recent research from home and abroad and to encourage teachers to be open to different ways of doing things, to be light-footed and, in particular, aware of the ways young people acquire and understand information. There should be a network of centres like this in schools across the country, driving evidence-based research.

This approach is not a licence, as some gainsayers would have it, to cast away the proven worth of traditional methods or, worse still, to 'dumb down' and reduce the potency of academic rigour. Far from it. Most successful companies have research and development functions embedded in their business strategy; schools do not. Reviewing and enhancing ways of working should be natural for any good professional.

I shudder when I think how little I appreciated any of this as a young and newly qualified teacher. There were some practical skills to be learnt, certainly, but no sense at all of continuing progress. My one-year PGCE gave me a ticket for life. What worries me now is that we have a generation of younger teachers who believe that their professional purpose is to meet defined assessment objectives – and no more, because nothing else seems to be valued. They know no better and we have allowed this to happen.

Visiting a state-maintained school recently, I observed a lesson given by an articulate, bright young man who had established a lively and effective rapport with his class. On all four walls of the classroom were bright orange notices. These strident notices, to which the young teacher referred with great frequency during the lesson, listed the assessment objectives for the course of study. The teacher was assiduous and knowledgeable: the children were in good hands, the assessment objectives were clear to everyone. Yet I forget what he was teaching them about.

Our society will be enriched if we imbue our teachers with a strong sense of the powerful potential of an holistic view of schooling, if we train them thoroughly, monitor them regularly and let them express their vocation to the full. In other words let them get on with it.

When it comes to hiring new teachers, the ones who seem merely to want a job I discard swiftly. The ones who impress as professionals likely to grow with their experience of the school are an altogether more attractive proposition. But there is something else I desire, though it is harder to find: vocation.

Just over a hundred years ago, A. C. Benson wrote that there should be 'a conscious consecration of self to work in school masters'. The pull of dedication, he thought, was more important than anything else. Making a fuss about the great call of vocation, however, was wrong in two particulars: first, because doing so was characteristically not English (well, this was Edwardian England), and second, because it is, in his word, 'priggish'. He goes on to say that there have been a great many school masters who have 'undeniably been prigs', characterized by a debilitating lack of humour. Top of the list in Benson's pantheon of great prig school masters was the celebrated Dr Arnold, about whom Benson says, 'the vigour of the man, his goodness, his simplicity shine out on every page of his biography, but I think that is easier to admire in a book than it would have been in real life'.

The vocation of which Benson speaks is having a belief in what one is doing but in a way that is 'rather deep and secret'. A man should quietly 'accept the inevitable failures of his life as lessons sent to himself to show that he cannot always be as effective as he would like to be'. Benson goes on to say that there is just as much a problem if the pendulum swings too far the other way, so that a school master might think of himself as only an ordinary professional, conscientious and uninspired. Benson's book is full of practical tips and observations, and he was clearly a talented classroom practitioner, but there is no doubt at all that he saw mere professionalism as a hollow sham. Vocation, quietly and profoundly expressed, was the bedrock of all.

How do we entice young people into teaching today? We challenge them to do something socially useful, and urge them to put themselves to the test professionally. The Department for Education 'Get Into Teaching' website is keen to advertise the benefits of a teaching career. It states that research shows teachers feel twice as *alert/happy/proud/ relaxed/involved* as professionals in IT, Accountancy or Marketing. This seems a rather half-hearted claim. Not only is this an approach that fails to identify *why* there is a 'natural high' for teachers in the classroom; it is self-referential. Sensibly enough, the website urges would-be teachers to speak to an old hand. Why? To find out about 'behaviour management, workload management, subject knowledge and curriculum'. No room here for soggy ideas about vocation or the energetic optimism, the love of learning and life willingly shared with pupils that distinguishes the best teachers. This glance at teaching's front-of-house web page illustrates just how absurd appears the old-fashioned Benson's high-sounding sanctimonious guff. It has been replaced by sharp-edged, clear-sighted and, above all, measurable professionalism.

And this is the pity of it. In what is now a quarter-century of head-mastering, I don't recall seeing such well-intentioned, talented young people venturing across the threshold of teaching. Yet I do not recall a generation who define their purpose as teachers in such a limited way.

I believe the effect of new-wave professionalism matters profoundly for the schools we are and wish to be. Teachers who increasingly see themselves as part of a professional body that delivers outcomes will end up as functionaries in a service industry. This is not a cry from a wild-eyed prophet hankering after a fictitious golden age. The rank amateurism of past years deserves no celebration. On my first day as a teacher, I was cornered by a physically substantial, older colleague who informed me that good teachers are born, not made, and that I should shape up or ship out. He then turned on his heel and waddled away. This was my formal induction to the mysteries and nuances of a complex art.

I see such enthusiasm and preparedness to engage among this new generation of young teachers that I believe each deserves the best encouragement to embrace a vocation. Whatever the pressures of measurement culture, it is the responsibility of heads to enable young teachers to feel their vocation as well as construct their professional career. In part this means celebrating their contribution as part of the great British liberal tradition of an holistic education, but, more importantly, it means encouraging them to see that it is through the building of good relationships with pupils and with colleagues that truly effective communities are created: schools that not only can deliver the highest grades but, vitally, can enable young people to learn to stand up both for themselves and for a purpose greater than themselves.

When I was a young teacher a rather fossilized older colleague was wont to bang on about the 'primacy of love'. We rather ignored him, not least because the language was slightly embarrassing. But he was right. And so was A. C. Benson. Great teachers use their heads but teach from the heart.

4

Adolescence

The notorious flogger Dr John Keate, Head Master of
Eton in the early part of the nineteenth century, became
a byword for the gross excesses of public schools. A
review in the *Manchester Guardian* describes Dr Keate as
a 'coarse ruffian'. In an age when the head might have to
deal with as many as two hundred boys single-handedly,
he would adopt a combative style and face them down.
Twice he felt obliged to call in the local militia to suppress
boy rebellion.

Yet in his retirement he was feted by his old boys.
Such retrospective hero status can be a consequence of a
romantic and selective memory, but in Keate's case it seems
it was more than that. The school was 'fondly attached
to him', he was the boys' 'surest friend', he was 'enemy to
none, and enemy he has not'. As a former pupil, Sir Francis
Doyle observed, 'he had no favourites, and flogged the son
of a duke and the son of a grocer with perfect impartiality'.
Consistency and fairness were qualities as much needed
by teenagers then as they are now.

Doyle goes on to make a telling comparison between Keate and man-of-the-age Dr Arnold. With high-mindedness and moral certainty, Dr Arnold sought to eradicate immorality and set the tone for a public school revolution that came to see sport, chapel and a prefectorial system of leadership as the way to create good men. But as Doyle observes,

> there was one qualification for a head master which Keate possessed but Arnold did not – having the knowledge of God Almighty's intention that there should exist for a certain time, between childhood and manhood, the natural progression known as a boy. He was rough with them I admit, but neither unkind nor unjust beneath that roughness. He was right hearted in the depths of his nature.

By comparison with the aloof, priggish Arnold, whose concern was the creation of men, Keate seemed at least to have recognized the natural progression we now term 'adolescence'.

Generally speaking, Arnold's response is more typical of the way society has viewed the teenage years. In past times, schooling, such as was available, was something to pass through as swiftly as possible so that teenagers could take their place as useful members of society. There are remarkable stories that attest to the capacity of young people to assume considerable responsibility, like the young teenage officers of the Royal Navy in the age of sail. Part of me has some sympathy with this view because in contemporary society we routinely underestimate what teenagers are capable of achieving. Yet it is a dangerous assumption to believe teenagers are just adults with less experience: as we shall see, the teenage years are a special and important time in human development.

In more recent times, the cult of the teenager has grown, often labelled 'youth culture'. It is really only in the last sixty years or so that teenagers have been identified as a social phenomenon, a group exhibiting particular behaviours and tastes. When it became apparent that this group offered a distinctive and valuable commercial market, they became a specific target for advertisers. It may be overstating the case to claim that the public conception of 'teenager' has largely been created by the profit motive, but the two are intimately linked. The more teenagers have been described as a tribe apart, as different creatures to adults, the less we seem to have understood what is happening to them. The pendulum has swung the other way: we too frequently see teenagers as aliens. It is common for parents to say that they cannot understand their child at all and seek help from anyone who can interpret their children's strange utterances or silences.

For most of my teaching career I have relied on intuition and common sense in dealing with teenagers. There has been little science to help guide us. Most of what teachers know is born of their own experience.

When I address parents of new pupils on the first day of the school year, I begin by observing that, in my experience, starting a school is usually tougher for the parents than the child. I also remind them about their own teenage years by referring to my memories of being a teenager, of being in turns off-hand and interested, surly and pleasant, enthusiastic and blasé, with all the uncertainty that bewildering changes of mood and aspiration bring. Of only one thing, incidentally, was I certain at that age: that I would never become a teacher. I then refer to a text. I read a passage from a book written by an Eton house master, John McConnell, in 1967. In it, he imagines the letter he wished he had written to all mothers on their son's fifteenth birthday. It has wisdom and intuitive truth. Long out of print, this passage deserves to be read:

Today is Tom's 15th birthday. You will be glad to hear that he received a nice bundle of envelopes and packages in the post this morning. The cake you ordered has arrived safely and I have given him leave to go home to lunch with you next Sunday.

However, the real purpose of this letter is to try and prepare you for an imminent change in the relationship between yourself and your son. The affectionate small boy who has quite justifiably been your pride and joy is about to undergo such a transformation that you may well begin to wonder whether you have mothered a monster. The piping treble voice, you will observe, has already begun to crack. The down on his cheeks and chin is stiffening into defiant bristles and there is an angry hue about the blemishes on his skin. Perhaps you have already started to wonder where you have gone wrong, and what you have done to deserve his new found anger. You, who have shown him most affection, will seem to be the butt for his most barbed and unkindly remarks. That is because you are still the most important woman in his life and the most convenient target for his burgeoning masculine aggressiveness.

Do not despair. Ride out the storm. Be firm but affectionate. At this moment when he seems to need you least, he needs you most. Make a stand about the principles you regard as fundamental. Give him rope about the less important things. Do not worry too much about his wearing apparel or the length of his hair. Comfort yourself with the knowledge that his present mood is transitory. If you do this and stand firm as a rock in the midst of his tempestuous life, the small boy whom you thought you had lost will return to you as a charming young man – well groomed in appearance and with delightful manners. He will have been worth waiting for.

Meanwhile, we are both of us in for one hell of a time.

Reading out this letter prepares the way for my attempt to describe to parents how we help shape things in school. It also offers reassurance. One of the best house masters I have known had a particular gift for being able to reduce difficult situations to manageable proportions: 'He will be fine' was his usual avuncular refrain to worried parents. The house master was a steady and gifted pastoral figure. He was often right, the teenager usually was indeed fine, but not always.

Herein lies the difficulty. In truth, professionals in school have had very little ability to comprehend the complexities and nuances of much of teenage behaviour. We have taken a broad-brush view in the hope that things will turn out well and we have tried our best to help, but we have not had the sure knowledge or justified confidence to support a particular course of action. The application of neuroscience to schooling will change all that. These are exciting times. The possibility is opening up that neuroscience will lighten our shadowy understanding.

I have been fortunate in having as my deputy at Eton Dr Bob Stephenson, a neuro-pharmacologist by training and a biology teacher by profession. He carries out all and more of the usual responsibilities of a deputy head and has a long-standing interest in neuroscience. His lecture on the landscape of adolescence has helped many parents make sense of what they see.

He observes that it is common for us all to believe that once our children reach adolescence somehow the huge gulf between childhood and adulthood has been bridged. We believe that we are dealing with an individual who, although perhaps physically still undergoing some development, has a brain that is fully matured, lacking perhaps a little experience, but nothing that a sound secondary education cannot provide. In fact, nothing could be further from the truth. There are huge differences between the way that the adult and adolescent brains operate. It should not surprise us that if the body lacks physical maturity then the brain must have a concomitant and parallel process of development taking place. A teenager appearing to behave like a lunatic may just be a normal adolescent. It is as though this is an evolutionary process designed to cause maximum frustration to parents, yet such processes have been carefully selected to ensure the most robust and successful outcome for the child (and, though it can sometimes be hard to believe, also for the parent).

Two thousand and more years ago, Socrates spoke disparagingly of teenagers:

> Our youth now love luxury. They have bad manners, contempt for authority; they show disrespect for their elders and love chatter in place of exercise; they no longer rise when elders enter their room; they contradict their parents, chatter before company, gobble up their food and tyrannize their teachers.

We may recognize many of the traits Socrates describes, as indeed did Keate. What we are beginning to learn is that for a child to become a decent citizen is not just a question of changing his immature social attitudes. There is now very good evidence that an adolescent's often inexplicable, and sometimes bizarre, behaviour is underpinned by complicated biological processes.

Psychologists have often viewed adolescence as a period of storm and stress. This need not be the case. It seems odd that for all our supposed sophistication in the measurement of academic achievement, we have largely disregarded the behaviour of the young people we are trying to help. It has been assumed for many years that good teachers would be sensitive to the needs and limitations of their pupils, and that educational principles that work for adults would, perhaps with some modification, be suitable for adolescents. Emerging neurobiological evidence shows that apparently simple concepts such as the motivation to learn and achieving academic engagement need careful consideration. This is not to say that past generations have got it all wrong or that a good teacher cannot circumvent many of the problems. Indeed, one of the most fascinating aspects of the unfolding scientific evidence is seeing how it supports and explains so much of the behaviour we have observed and sometimes endured.

At 10 years of age children are delightful, living in the happy knowledge that they are the centre of the universe created by their parents, and that by and large they do not have to venture far away from their little world. They feel safe and secure within it. Suddenly, and in a matter of months, they are driven by something within themselves to explore a world outside of this egocentric universe that they have created and are forced to seek out new roles and identities for themselves. Some of these new personality profiles and explorations of behaviour work and are stable, but the vast majority are not and are only transient flashes of a programme that in itself has a limited lifespan.

It is hard for us to imagine or remember well what it was really like to live through adolescence. Indeed there may be very good biological and practical reasons why these memories have been expunged. Nevertheless, imagine a dream such as this: you are hurtling along a country road in a vehicle that seems vastly over-powered and with a braking system that is clearly inadequate. The accelerator appears to have a mind of its own and is fully depressed spontaneously when any other car tries to overtake you. The path ahead is unclear, the windscreen is murky and there are many possible routes to take along the way. The promised rewards at the end of the journey are huge and although the instinct to stop the car is sometimes desirable, you know that there is no turning back. This is the picture of adolescence that is emerging. At some levels it seems a troubling and frightening journey, but at others it offers an enormously exciting and productive phase of life.

The last 15 years have seen an almost exponential rise in the neurobiological evidence available to support psychological investigation; most notably the ease with which magnetic resonance scans can be performed is producing a wealth of data. This throws light not only upon the structural transformations in the brain but also, by being able to monitor blood flow in the brain, on those regions that are active when particular tasks are being performed. In particular, it illustrates the connections that are being established between discrete regions of the brain.

Yet there is need for a warning. As with any new technological advance, the results of the technology are sometimes pounced upon by popular writers as proof that there are natural centres for religion, homosexuality etc. This is not a new phenomenon. In the early days of genetic studies into schizophrenia, when single genes were posited for this terrible disease, simplistic models were produced indicating that it runs in families. Genetic explanations were not produced, nor indeed even looked for, which allowed a theory to gain traction that was as credible as claiming that poverty runs in families. The basic science needs to be clearly established, relating any evidence from new technologies to what has already painstakingly been established through other research.

The studies with adolescence started with excellent structural analysis demonstrating clearly and rather surprisingly that there are huge changes in the structure of the cerebral cortex which are not complete until subjects reach their late twenties. For parents who are just embarking upon their children's teenage years, the news is that this intriguing, fascinating, challenging and sometimes bumpy ride does not end until a male is aged about 28. When I have revealed this information in front of parents, mothers tend to disbelieve that it is only age 28; many claim that the person they married is still an adolescent.

There are both progressive and regressive changes in the brain. The former include:

- neurogenesis (the growth and branching of nerve cells),
- synaptogenesis (the making of new connections) and
- growth of myelin (the insulation of long-fibre tracts for rapid transmission).

Growth and progression are perhaps what one might have expected, but at least as important are the regressive changes. These include cell death and synaptic pruning. The synapses spread out many times like the branches of a tree; some of these branches are used regularly, others are not, and the ones that are not will wither, they are 'pruned'. In part this process is pre-programmed but it is also intimately related to usage (on the 'Use it or lose it' principle). This feature is well established in neurobiology. An interesting piece of work was conducted in the 1980s on the mechanism that changes the ability of Japanese babies to detect the difference between R and L sounds (a well-known phenomenon when listening to Japanese people speak English). Japanese babies who were not exposed to subtle distinctions in these sounds during a critical nine-month period lost the ability to identify and articulate them. This does not mean it is impossible to learn the distinction, but the facility to do so is impaired through the loss of critical pathways and the techniques required to learn may be unusual and difficult.

The continuing importance of cell death as a key element in adolescence, and indeed throughout life, is perhaps surprising, but it has major implications for the way we learn. Disturbances to these malleable systems during critical periods of adolescence can have significant impact. There is a massive, natural surge of synaptic growth just before the onset of puberty and another prominent period of synaptic pruning and plasticity during adolescence. In some brain regions up to half of the synaptic connections are eliminated. The picture we have then is of the sculptor starting out with a partially shaped block of marble: the quality of the final piece will depend upon a range of influences with a myriad of different possibilities – but only rudimentary features will be visible in the original block of stone.

The total brain size is approximately 90 per cent of its adult size at the age of 6. Generally, basic motor and sensory functions mature more quickly than higher-order functions like decision-making and exercising control. Nine- and ten-year-olds soak up sensory experience like a sponge in an undirected way. From puberty onwards children are driven to channel and direct this sensory experience to gain sharp feedback. This feedback can be positive (appetitive) or negative (aversive); in many ways it does not matter which, as it is having the reward of feedback that matters. Teenagers can sometimes appear 'black and white' in their responses, as though they are pushing for a reaction, and they are – naturally so.

Structural magnetic resonance imaging (MRI) shows grey matter loss (pruning) earliest in the sensorimotor cortex and latest in the dorsolateral prefrontal cortex. It is this late pruning of the frontal cortex that is most interesting. These regions are involved in the higher-order integration of information needed for planning, strategizing and goal-setting, activities that require the ability to focus attention and exert control over behaviour. Most importantly the *connections* between these important frontal cortex regions and the structures below which stimulate appetitive (striatum) and aversive behaviours (amygdala) are very immature and have poor links with the memory (hippocampus).

The picture we have then is that of the motor driving behaviour forward and being only loosely integrated with those higher functions that allow subtle differentiation about the appropriate action to take. The engine is powering away, but the selection of gears and indicators and use of the brake can appear randomly applied. As we shall see, this has profound implications not only for the growing adolescent body, but also for a teenager's perception of social behaviour.

In itself this may not seem a problem. After all, if this development was a linear process all we would see would be an increasing level of control developing and thus more mature behaviour. However, it is not a linear process and there is one important area that is changing at a rapid rate from the start of adolescence. Parents are familiar with the impulsivity of young children and their inability to differentiate between the relative importance of different things. We hold their hands as we walk along the pavement and restrain them from rushing across the road to pat the neighbour's dog when there is a 10-ton truck hurtling towards them. But we tend to have little patience with young people who jump off the edge of a cliff for a dare, take ecstasy for the hell of it, or engage in a raft of risky behaviours. Taking such risks has been well observed in the literature surrounding adolescence, both scientific and cultural, and it tends to be attributed to poor education or a sudden hormonally driven rush of blood to the head. Yet in reality it is a manifestation of a carefully defined evolutionary process which is selected to drive the sculpturing of the higher centres of the brain.

Evolutionarily speaking, adolescence is a period of gaining independence from the immediate protection of the family, which simultaneously may occasionally put the individual in harm's way. Such independence-seeking behaviours are observed across mammalian species, with increases in peer-directed behaviour and the growing attraction of novelty being reflected in adolescents' propensity for risky behaviour. In scientific terms, this risky behaviour may be defined as the product of immature control systems in the frontal lobes and a very powerful motor in the striatum driving a search for stimulus and reward. This developmental pattern is likely to be an evolutionary feature: an individual 'needs' to engage in high-risk behaviour to leave a safe and familiar environment in order to find an identity and find a mate and procreate. Expressed in this logical way, it seems a straightforward enough business, but it is surprising how hard this is for so many young people and their parents. The over-powered car is hurtling towards the unknown with a very inadequate braking system.

But what of the fuzzy windscreen? When the prefrontal networks are not fully mature there is a greater chance adolescents will need to maximize these resources when engaging in tasks that engage prefrontal activity. Additional stressors in the environment, whether unexpected or ongoing (family, social, or illness problems, for example), can lead to impaired behaviour. The frontal lobes are overloaded and interpretation of stimuli may well now reside in subcortical structures such as the amygdala. Put simply, when your son is preoccupied with other matters, perhaps the breaking up of a relationship or the knowledge that poor results in examinations are about to be exposed, his hostile or strange response to your simple question has a scientific explanation. It is rather unnerving to have your polite enquiry greeted by the aggressive retort, 'Why are you looking at me like that?' when as far as you were concerned you were just expressing gentle parental concern.

The fuzzy windscreen describes the distorted perception of the adolescent without the normal crystal filter of unburdened frontal lobes. The business of dealing with adolescents is complicated by the fact that their routes can be so very different. Some parents will say that they never see any of these apparent difficulties, and therein lies the rub. The sculpturing of the frontal lobes and the stable integration of other systems with them could be relatively seamless and sometimes is. The shifting of balance towards more frontal lobe control is considered by most now to be the biological basis of maturation. For example, the development of effective self-regulation – the ability to delay gratification of immediate reward in order to follow the rules, make appropriate choices, and maintain goals – depends heavily upon the development of the networks involved in cognitive control.

Neuroscientists are now making significant progress in identifying these networks and developing strategies to maximize the social experience required for such stable integration. However, what is clear is that it is absolutely essential to allow adolescents to make mistakes; to experience the bizarre, but to allow them to do it in a safe environment which allows them to get things wrong and learn from the experience.

Structural measurements of cortical grey matter and measurement of the subtle psychological implications of the changes that occur both tend to support a theory which is supported by functional MRI studies showing the engagement of particular regions of the brain: the adolescent brain is less able than an adult's to deal with changes in the rules of a particular task or to inhibit behaviour and is more sensitive to reward.

What about the accelerator being depressed further when a following car tries to overtake? The adolescent is particularly sensitive to the presence of peers and the influence of peer groups. For example, in simulated driving games when the object of the exercise is to get to the end of a hazardous course in the quickest possible time, the mere knowledge that the subject's peer group is observing alters performance in the adolescent group, but not the adult group. The adolescents take more risks completing the course. This result is reflected in greater activity in the striatum and frontal cortex, changing the potential value of the reward for risky decisions. The effect is particularly notable in those who are concerned about how others see them. As parents we want to trust our children when they have just passed their driving tests to be responsible when going out for a night with their friends. We worry about alcohol and not much about their friends. In practice, the current generation of teenagers has heeded the lesson not to drink and drive rather better than their parents' generation. The potential for real danger is being in the company of their friends. While I would be happy for teenagers to drive themselves to school, under no circumstances would I allow them to give a lift to friends. And I would not buy the argument that they 'concentrate better' with blaring, loud music filling the car.

Humans are an immensely social species. We create friendships, love relationships, family units, social groups, societies and cultures. Our brains have developed specialized networks to receive and process social information. These networks allow us to recognize others, to be aware of their perspectives and to evaluate their desires, beliefs and intentions. In short, to be a successful human we all need to be 'natural psychologists' with an ability to decide in an instant how to proceed in a social situation. This is known as theory of mind or mentalizing.

As adolescents move away from their immediate family group, their reliance upon the frontal lobes to integrate information from the memory becomes increasingly demanding and they are not initially very good at it. Having spent much of my teaching career in boarding schools, it has been a fascinating experience to observe how 10 boys thrust together at the age of 13 in a boarding house negotiate the myriad complexities involved in creating a stable and integrated group. The scientist sees how each individual with his uniquely emerging sculptured neural system copes with the social group. As a teacher, I am interested to see how some groups develop the strongest of bonds (all 10 boys choosing to go on holiday together, for example), while other groups stutter and sometimes become dysfunctional.

Boarding has a unique place in the acceleration of these processes. For example, increased time spent with peers can lead to new social skills and increased social support. Similarly, being part of a group increases desire for novelty, excitement and risk-taking, which can lead to opportunities to explore adult behaviour and to becoming more adept at negotiating the challenges of life. Parents asking about the importance of this group experience are sometimes surprised with the reply that it is the 'provision of controlled chaos'. The boarding environment provides a unique opportunity to test out many different identities, and reactions to them, with little or no harm being done to the family unit in this sometimes volatile process. However, the success of the education depends upon both the robustness and sensitivity of the buffer. Teenagers can and, indeed, must kick against institutional structures and rules but in turn these must be devised with clear boundaries based on an understanding of what drives teenagers' behaviour.

The challenge for educators is to embrace neurobiological research and enter into a new contract with the young. This is not to say that heads should mitigate punishment for unacceptable behaviour if the culprit pleads that he had no control over his behaviour – 'It wasn't me, sir, it was my brain.' Nevertheless I do have some sympathy with the boy appearing before me for a disciplinary infringement who has acted in a bizarre way and who replies to the question, 'Why did you do it?' with the retort, 'I don't know, sir.' This may sound like the perfect defence to avoid further painful scrutiny, but in fact it is quite likely that he genuinely does not know. It is not surprising, given a combination of underdeveloped interactions between frontal lobes and motivational systems, peer pressure, parental expectation and physical development, that the path ahead is blurred!

Given the heterogeneity among brains and the range of different developmental experiences it is a wonder that adults can communicate effectively at all. Indeed sometimes one might wonder if we are doing so! It is much more complicated to communicate with an adolescent when we are dealing with an individual whose brain is not yet fully developed. The experienced teacher lives and breathes in this world, continuously altering their approach to situations to allow the learning environment to be the most effective. Understanding the brain mechanisms that underlie learning and memory could transform what we do in the classroom. In educational circles it is fashionable to suggest that much of what we do will be replaced by clever interactive computer programmes. While I have no doubt that there will be some useful development in this area, I also have no doubt that learning is at its most effective when it is transmitted with human social contact.

One caveat to the 'use it or lose it' idea proposed earlier is *how* you use it. Japanese children who had moved through the critical window of development for the R and L sounds were capable of recovering function provided that when they were exposed to the material again it was delivered to them by a different person. Video of the same human was not sufficient, nor was the sound alone. The material delivered was exactly the same, but the live experience influenced the development of the pathways. We are now discovering that mechanisms that can stimulate the striatum before material is learnt can have powerful effects upon the learning of that event. Understanding these processes will allow teachers to investigate new ways to stimulate academic engagement.

In all of this the attitudes and opinions of our children cannot and should not be ignored. This difference in perspective is neatly summarized by Mark Twain: 'When I was a boy of fourteen, my father was so ignorant I could hardly stand to have the old man around. But when I got to be twenty-one, I was astonished at how much he had learned in seven years.' I am constantly amazed at how much the adolescent can tell us: simply observing them can allow us to have a window into their world. A few years ago a senior member of the Facebook team came to talk to boys, no doubt to gain a valuable perspective on the adolescent mind. A teenager asked the question, 'How would it be if every time you bought something online this information was transmitted to your friends on Facebook?' The suggestion appalled me, as it was such an invasion of privacy, but this question sent a buzz of excitement around the room which defied belief. This apparently was the holy grail. If you have been the recipient of an email or text from your child when they are sitting in their room in the same building as you, you may wonder quite where the world is heading. Indeed the proliferation and popularity of social networking among the young is frightening to parents.

Yet this kind of faceless contact may make good sense to them. By any definition of human society it is impossible to have 3,000 friends, but a sample of 3,000 people on whom to try out myriad identities is relatively painless and possibly beneficial. Several studies have shown that adolescent self-reports of their sensitivity to acceptance and rejection by their peers are much higher than those of both children and adults. In adolescents how they appear to their peer group was more important than in other age groups for determining their self-worth. Given their immaturity of social cognition, instant feedback in social media is perhaps both necessary and valuable to the adolescent.

We need to ask whether online social networking has any correspondence with the way people connect face to face. It has already been established that as a learning tool it probably does not, but it may buffer the adolescent from some of the more painful moments that can occur in peer groups by circumnavigating some of the awkwardness that comes from their poor ability to read social situations. There can be no doubt, however, that adolescents report more distress when they feel socially isolated than do adults and children. We simply do not know enough about the way young people interact on social networks to answer some of these questions, but what is striking is the way these communications change and the intuitive cyber-cognition that is emerging so that emotional cues are perceived more accurately than we might ever have imagined. As with many parents, my brain is not attuned to it and I am well beyond the developmental window.

A number of important points emerge. The default mode of adults is to talk at young people in the belief that imparting wisdom is at the heart of the educational process. We can learn much more by listening and discussing what we do not know. Time spent listening to teenage children is valuable time. You will certainly learn many things that you do not know and perhaps did not want to know, but at least there is a platform for a dialogue. As we have discovered, the modus operandi of the adolescent brain is to avoid emotionally charged issues; when faced with them the result can be explosive and worrying. Difficult topics are best engaged through regular communication without judgement being given.

However, there is a more profound and important educational point to make here. Throughout my years as a teacher I have never ceased to be amazed by the creativity and flexibility of the adolescent mind. It is one of the joys of being a teacher. Unfortunately the conventional world of education stifles this. Our society's almost doctrinal emphasis upon deductive reasoning, convergent thinking and selective retention perversely excludes divergent thinking, approximation and, importantly, guessing. If we are truly to understand the adolescent mind and develop effective ways to minimize the effects of risk-taking behaviour, we really need to understand these processes and engage with them. There is no logic involved with drug-taking and gambling. Adults can learn, too; understanding these mechanisms will also allow us to encourage creativity and value the spontaneity so characteristic of the adolescent mind.

Practical tips for parents

When facing stressful moments, it can help to remember that, in a neurological sense, your adolescent child is, quite literally, not all there. In particular:

1. Keep up regular conversations, however resistant your teenager may be. These should be a natural part of life and not a special event when a problem crops up.

2. If talking at home is a problem, think about a different venue. A car journey with just the two of you and no eye contact allows a low-key, unthreatening conversation. It is surprising how much is revealed in a car!

3. Honesty is key. Be consistent.

4. Especially with boys, deal with one issue at a time. On no account allow yourself to be fired up and say, 'And another thing…'

5. Remember that teenage identity is not fixed: an attitude or behaviour may well change.

6. Avoid generalizations, especially about friends.

7. Get to know your teenager's friends.

8. Listen!

9. Stay resilient; teenagers let you down – repeatedly, but they need you to be there.

10. However frustrating they are, criticize their behaviour, not them. They may try to shrug it off, but adolescents really need to feel loved.

5

Sex, Drugs and Rock 'n' Roll

As we have seen, the impulses that drive adolescence are not rooted in logic, but release spontaneity and a desire to experiment. It is a function of adolescence to experiment by breaking free from the bonds of childhood and family.

Ian Drury's song 'Sex & Drugs & Rock & Roll', released in 1977, is about breaking free from the mundane, although it very rapidly became known as a punk anthem celebrating excess. To worried parents it sounds like an adolescent charter. At a time when their children are pushing the boundaries and experimenting, somewhere in sex, drugs and teenage culture lies the stuff of parents' nightmares.

Sex

As parents we want our children to lead healthy, balanced lives, to experience delight and comfort in their relationships. We have some memory of the confusion, ignorance and self-doubt of adolescent sexuality, but that memory does not equip us to deal with our children; indeed, it can add to a parent's confusion: just what should I say? The best advice, though this is frequently a challenge, is to talk openly about the naturalness of sex.

Parents tell me they have three principal worries: how to deal with under-age sex, the pervasiveness of pornography, and homosexuality.

The pressure on young teenagers, especially girls, to be sexually active seems to have grown exponentially, stoked by the internet and social media. It is a muddling business. For a young girl, in particular, there may be no physical drive at all, but being told by peers that failing to participate in some form of sex game is pathetic can prove incentive enough. Torn between their parents' anxiety and what their peers might think, it is their peers who often win. How much easier it is to go along with it in the belief that your parents will never know.

There is a strong argument for supportive sex education to be taught to children well before they reach secondary school age. It is a difficult balance to strike. As a parent I would wish my child to enjoy an innocent view of life for as long as possible, but I would not want her to be pressurized into something she did not wish to do through her own ignorance. Explaining the mechanics of sex is one thing; putting it in context is harder and, in some ways, more important.

By the age of 13 boys and girls need to have open conversations with adults about sex to establish facts which will feed their burgeoning curiosity. Without the facts it is striking what myths are peddled: that there are no attendant health risks to a promiscuous young boy or girl, for example, or that oral sex is not sexual activity. There are hard truths, too, such as knowing that sexual activity with multiple partners increases the risk of disease. It is also crucial to discuss another possibility: saying no. There can be palpable relief in some young people, boys as much as girls, when it is explained that it is normal and healthy to have no sexual relationships as a teenager. The backwash from our commendable desire to explain the benefits of safe sex is that the impression is given that sexual activity is the norm.

The skill involved in developing loving relationships merits as much discussion as the science of sex. This seldom happens in schools. Teachers feel on dangerous territory: biology is safer. One good topic for conversation, at school or at home, is the legal age of consent. Why is there a legal age of consent at all and why is it 16? Most young teenagers will respond well to this debate and though views will vary will show good sense in appreciating how laws can protect and enhance individual choice. In the same vein, the common sense of parental 'laws' can offer fruitful discussion: why you will or will not allow your child to sleep with a boy/girl friend in your house, for example. (I would say absolutely not, under the age of 18.) In the dodgem-car world of adolescent logic, explaining why rules exist is necessary; reasons obvious to a parent may not appear that way to them at all.

Parenting styles tend to be described as stereotypes, either autocratic or a pushover. There is a third way: research shows that parents who hold a line, but regularly discuss the reasons behind their decisions, raise adolescents who are more confident, poised and self-reliant – and less susceptible to peer pressure. For an adolescent, simply being told no is unlikely to work in the long run.

The ease of access to pornography is astonishing. Vast swathes of the internet are given over to it. Parents frequently ask how worried they should be. Teenage boys, in sensible conversation, say they can differentiate between the images and the reality. They are curious, pornography is exciting, but they do not read it as a textbook for relationships. In many cases this will be true. Rather as with the 1960s argument about cartoon violence contaminating the young, there is no evidence to link the two decisively. But repeated use of pornography does influence attitudes, especially in the arena of social media and texting. The potential for harm comes not so much from the material as from buying in to the underlying values.

A 14-year-old boy emails his girlfriend of the same age some photographs of young women in provocative poses. The pictures excite him, so he assumes they will excite her and encourage her to send him pictures of herself. The communication is interrupted by a parent and the police are immediately contacted. To the astonishment of the boy his behaviour falls under paedophile laws and a lengthy investigation ensues. The incident is interesting on several levels. It gives some insight into the logic of a 14-year-old boy, it illustrates the fear active in parents' minds, and it points to heavy-handedness in the application of the law. Above all, it serves to demonstrate why behaviour around sex needs to be discussed.

How should a parent react when catching their child, usually a boy, with pornography? I would take the opportunity to talk about the matter openly, about distinguishing between fantasy and reality, about his frequency of use, but I would try not to make him feel guilty and I would not ban his computer.

Most boys will move on: it becomes boring and real relationships with people they like assume a much greater significance. In a small number of cases the boy will become fixated, even addicted. Addiction is much more likely to be seen in a solitary, isolated, socially anxious adolescent for whom pornography creates a world apart. If social activities go by the wayside and he becomes reclusive, it may be a sign of addiction. The approach should be broadly the same, but in this case, restrictions on access to computers and social media are necessary. To a gambling addict even losing feels good. To a porn addict no barriers will be sufficient to deter him. He needs professional help. For most young people an interest in pornography is natural curiosity. The truth is that we parents tend to give pornography a clear run because we do not talk about sex and relationships enough.

The virtue of honest talk also applies to homosexuality. In times to come I suspect people will look back and wonder that so much fuss was made about something so straightforward. Yet the possibility that a son or a daughter might be homosexual exercises many parents mightily. In particular some parents worry that their child might be drawn to homosexuality by experiment. All the homosexuals I know say they were aware about feeling different around the age of 7 years old: sexual orientation is something natural and innate. A teenager will worry about it because he or she is frightened of the reactions of family and friends. For some it is a hard thing to accept and what they most need is support. Your child may be trying to come to terms with an uncertain future, with no prospect of a conventional family or children, for example. Schools, my own included, struggle to talk about homosexuality effectively because we do not yet know enough about how adolescent development affects perception, motivation and emotional stability. Be that as it may, from the teenager's point of view, it often feels as though nobody is telling them how they can deal with the situation.

School culture has changed over the years and mostly for the better. When a boy feels confident enough publicly to state that he is homosexual, other boys tend to respond positively and supportively. They recognize a fellow human being coming to terms with an important aspect of his life. That warm, personal response does not necessarily deter the same boys from using crass, homophobic language in

SEX, DRUGS AND ROCK 'N' ROLL

a casual way. Some teachers can be guilty, too, of failing to pick up and deal with this kind of language.

Social attitudes are a work in progress. In accepting homosexuality as part of the human condition we still have some way to go.

Drugs

We are all susceptible to drugs, be it a surfeit of caffeine or a dependence on aspirin. As adults, our experience and capacity for restraint will tend to shield us from the temptations of drugs that will do us harm. When it comes to drugs, assuming that an adult perception applies to the life of a teenager is misleading. We need to face facts.

- Fact 1: The considerable majority of teenagers will be involved in one way or another with potentially harmful drugs.

- Fact 2: Most parents don't want to believe it, so don't.

These bold statements may seem unduly alarmist but they are born of experience in schools watching how families deal with their children. The assertion that most teenagers will be involved in some way is not to suggest that they will be necessarily at risk of lasting harm or teetering on the edge of ruin, but they are highly likely to be offered recreational drugs at parties, in the street, even in the school or at a friend's home.

It is hard to describe what is out there. A particular challenge for parents and schools is having any hope of keeping abreast of the substances available, still less of the fast-changing street language that describes them. 'Weed' sounds comfortingly old-fashioned: names like billy, ram, tab, scag and mushies sound more exotic, but they are already out of date.

The substances most commonly used and abused by teenagers tend to fall into three broad groups:

- depressants (including alcohol, tranquillizers and inhaling volatile substances such as cigarette lighter fluid);

- stimulants (including nicotine, amphetamine and cocaine, as well as hallucinogens such as cannabis);

- and narcotics (notably heroin).

They all have the capacity to be harmful. Squirting fluid from an aerosol into the back of the throat, for example, has led to 130 teenage deaths in the UK in one year alone. We should disabuse ourselves of some of the myths too. The gentle soothing earthy cannabis from memories of the 1970s has been replaced by a far stronger version which, at higher doses, produces reactions from anxiety to panic paranoia and even psychosis. There is now evidence that persistent use of cannabis can cause permanent damage to nerve connections in the brain, leading to problems of learning, motivation and even personality. There is no safe nor easy drug.

Your children may tell you that so called 'legal highs' are all right; after all, they are legal. This group is the most frightening of the lot. The only reason many of them are not illegal is because they are new compounds, developed to make a fast buck, and the law has yet to catch up with them. Legal highs such as cannabinoids (spice) and mephedrone (meow meow) were made illegal in December 2009 and April 2010 respectively. There is a bewildering array of these legal highs on the market and no limit to the ingenuity of back-street chemists. Think of *Breaking Bad*. An illustration of the growing sophistication of this market is the quality of packaging for some of these drugs – cheerful, bright, welcoming and professional. There is serious money to be made.

These newly devised compounds are untested and untried. Although teenagers cannot know the provenance of a street drug – is it pure or adulterated with, say, brick dust? – they will have at least some idea about what the drug is. In the case of legal highs, however, they have no idea what is in it at all, which chemicals have been thrown together to create a new compound.

Parents have good cause to be worried. Legal highs play on the adolescent craving for new sensation and experiment. As parents and teachers we seek to give teenagers the opportunity to explore new possibilities and to allow them freedom, but in the knowledge that there is a safety net to catch them. With legal highs our children walk on the tightrope with no net.

It is not my aim to offer a scientific essay on drugs: the detail is readily available elsewhere. My aim is to suggest what parents should be looking for, what they should do and how schools can help.

Early signs of drug-taking may include changes of mood, sleeping late and slovenly appearance or an untidy room. These symptoms, as many parents would readily recognize, are also features of normal adolescence. On more than one occasion I have heard a highly vexed teenager expressing outrage that one of his parents mistakenly accused him of substance abuse, when as far as he was concerned he was being himself. At this point the frustration on both sides is evident and there is little real communication between the two.

The first tip to parents is to know what normal is. With teenagers 'normal' shifts and changes: parents need to be attuned to these changes. It is marked deviations from normal behaviour that should trigger concern. It is well worth finding time to talk to your teenager's friends, not conducting an inquisition, far less hectoring, but listening to them talk about what they like to do. You are likely to find out more about teenage subculture from your child's friends than from him or her.

In particular, be alert to excessive spending or borrowing of money. Experience shows that this is the surest sign. There will be other indications in the course of daily life: a marked decline in performance at school, lack of appetite, excessive tiredness without an apparent cause, unusual outbreaks of temper, restlessness and irritability. There can be physical signs too, such as sores or rashes, especially on the mouth or nose, or increased susceptibility to infection. And beware of attempts to cover up by using scents and colognes or wearing sunglasses.

Tell-tale signs can also be seen among your child's possessions or in the detritus of his room. Some of these will perhaps be obvious indicators, such as syringes and needles or spoons discoloured by heat, cigarette papers and lighters, spent matches or metal tins. But drugs come in many shapes and sizes, so parents need at least to question the appearance of small plastic bottles and metal foil wrappers, even sugar lumps and twists of paper. Some objects may indicate use of a particular drug: plastic bags and butane gas containers (solvent abuse), cardboard tubes or paper folded to form a small envelope (heroin), shredded cigarettes and cigarette papers (cannabis). The apparently least worrying items are the attractive, bright, rather childish stickers or transfers you might find lying around, but they could well be the vehicle for 'legal highs'.

The list is long and can seem endless. A parent will be forgiven for concluding that every item in a child's room might be an indication of something going terribly wrong. Your worries may be unfounded but it is better to have open conversations earlier on, however awkward, than face far greater problems further down the line.

There are some basic, perhaps obvious, steps to take if you have a worry.

1. Talk to your child when you are calm and he or she is receptive.

2. Stay calm and try to ascertain the truth at an early stage. Think carefully about what you are going to say and remember that you would not be having the conversation if you were not worried.

3. Teenagers can be very sophisticated and will convince you that there is nothing to worry about. Read up on the facts and be prepared to follow things through. Remember there is no such thing as a safe psychoactive substance.

4. It can be a good idea to have the conversation with another adult present or a sibling who may also be worried. The fact that you are both sharing concern may register with your child and jolt him back to reality. It is quite possible that he may not even be aware that he is displaying alarming symptoms.

5. Do not ask why he is taking drugs. This is not the real issue at this stage, nor is the fact that he is letting you down. He must trust you and be able to respond to your concern. It is quite possible that he has already recognized he is going too far and may have longed for such a conversation which could prove an escape route from peer pressure.

6. At this stage, your child may well feel able to tell you that he is involved in drugs. You can then work together to make progress. Clear guidelines from

you about what you think about drugs will help. If your child continues to deny that he is taking drugs, he should not mind having a test for them. The school or your doctor should be able to help. Indeed, your child's school should be a major support.

Whether or not to contact your teenager's school with a drug concern is a major worry in itself for most parents. From a head's point of view the single greatest issue in dealing with teenage drug problems is the reluctance of parents to work collaboratively with the school. Either the school is seen as a faceless institution that somehow is out to get the child or, usually more likely, parents are worried about what other people might think and keep quiet. There is a much greater chance of success if drug matters are raised early and faced up to.

Which brings us to the issue of trust. Parents need to trust the school, but the school needs to earn that trust. Parents would have every reason to be wary of contacting the school if the school adopts a heavy-handed policy. Years ago, like many heads, I adopted a straightforward cordon sanitaire policy: any suggestion of drugs and the child was expelled. It was the kind of robust no-nonsense policy parents like until it affects their own child. It became clear that this kind of simplistic approach has major drawbacks, not least in ensuring that nobody in the school community is prepared to talk about what is going on for fear of compromising a child and ruining their school career.

Yet teenagers need clarity. Adolescents need to have parameters of behaviour with sanctions that are consistently applied. Grey areas are confusing and reinforce the belief that rules are negotiable and really designed for other people.

Over the years at Eton we have developed a twin-track approach which, we have felt, is a step forward. Clarity comes from the understanding that any pupil caught using, selling or possessing drugs will automatically be expelled. The line is held firm. When a parent, teacher or a friend might have a concern about the pupil, a different route is taken. A conversation involving the pupil can take place in the knowledge that we are not in disciplinary territory. If the boy admits to involvement in drugs, the likely outcome is signing a contract, rather like signing a temperance pledge, by which he commits to a new path and willingly submits to random drug testing. If a subsequent test were to prove positive, he would have to leave the school.

A contract signed with the full agreement of the boy and his parents offers a supervised, supportive way ahead and, as it has proved, is often a relief to the teenager. It took some while for this contract route to be accepted and understood, but it has undoubtedly helped some boys make a success of their school careers as they have attested once they have moved on to university. From time to time boys themselves have asked to go on a contract. Over the years, I have been struck by the desire of most teenagers to have their lives under control: experiment is attractive but also frightening. It may not be possible for a teenager to articulate the thought, but shape and structure are reassuring.

Some parents have asked me why we do not introduce compulsory random drug testing for all. To me such an action would cut to the heart of trust in a school community. We are not running a police state and we are not trying to catch teenagers out. As in so many ways with teenagers, the trick is to find a balance between clear rules and responsiveness to the individual.

The twin-track route has had the advantage of opening up conversation. I have been grateful when a parent has shared their concerns about what is happening at teenage parties involving my pupils. It has allowed us to initiate conversations which may well lead nowhere and may well prove groundless, but which just may help or even save a child.

Drink

One drug mentioned under 'depressants' is worthy of a special footnote. Alcohol.

In some respects, dealing with alcohol is more complex than dealing with drugs as an issue in school. It is possible to have a considered and clear policy on drugs, rather less certain when it comes to alcohol. This is for two reasons: the adult world gives teenagers very mixed messages about alcohol and, in any event, the scientific message is itself mixed.

Double standards abound. A boy brings a bottle of vodka into his boarding house, with inevitable consequences. His father is outraged that the school allowed him to acquire the bottle until it is pointed out that the boy took it from his father's stash at home; a parent and school governor celebrates her daughter's leavers ball by bringing in crates of alcohol, which is liberally distributed to the teenagers, with, once again, inevitable consequences; a father provides cases of beer to his son's cricket team, all of which is drunk in short order by boys who drive themselves home, with, in this case, near-fatal consequences. It is in the area of alcohol more than any other that relationships between family and school can be under strain. Some parents, driven by an immature desire to be seen as matey or cool in the eyes of their teenage child's friends, behave irresponsibly and sometimes make a public show of defying the school's rules, claiming that the school goes over the top: 'It's just a rite of passage', they would say. 'Why such a fuss?'

It is a fuss because there is a very considerable difference between learning to drink moderately and healthily, and causing harm to yourself; between cafe culture and a nihilistic pleasure in binge-drinking.

When teaching teenagers about the effects of alcohol it is important to stick to the science. There is a great deal that can be said about the effect of alcohol on the gastrointestinal system, on the liver, on the pancreas and kidney, and on the cardiovascular system. There is also a great deal that can be said about its effect on the brain. But it is also important to show that alcohol brings some benefits, such as decreasing the blockage of blood vessels. Light drinking has also been shown to reduce the risk of a first heart attack and decrease the risk of a second. At the first stage, teenagers need to know the facts based on science. This is the line to take within the family. The continental habit of encouraging younger children to drink watered wine brings the moderated use of alcohol into the regular family environment. Alcohol is thus neither demonized nor subversively glamorous.

While this approach makes good sense, adolescents don't necessarily read or respond to good sense. They try to experiment, will cause problems and, odd though it may sound, I would far rather teenagers find out about themselves and their tolerance of alcohol in the controlled environment of a school than run greater risks later on. For many teenagers the business of being unpleasantly and embarrassingly drunk is enough for them to wish never to repeat the experience. Repeat offences for alcohol-related incidents raise different issues. Either the teenager has some propensity to alcohol, quite possibly linked to an addictive personality, or the failure to heed warnings bespeaks another issue altogether, quite possibly to do with self-worth and unhappiness. In either eventuality the school can offer support but will also need to hold a

disciplinary line. I would take the view that a third serious
alcohol offence should forfeit a place in the school.

Teenage culture

As adolescents begin the natural process of experimenting
with relationships and kicking against family bonds, they
will place increasing faith in a culture they feel is created by
their peers: a world of teenage slang, contrary perceptions
of the world and sometimes rebellious behaviour. In fact
this world is likely to be the product of external influences,
especially via the internet, but it will 'feel' their own, unique
to their group – and is certainly nothing to do with their
parents. From the age of 13 onwards, parents and school
need to make a conscious effort to introduce young people
to broad, social, adult culture, not in an attempt to suppress
teenage identity but to illustrate another perspective taken
from life outside the family.

There are various ways in which this can be achieved.
Experience of paid work, however menial and however
lowly the wage, is important to gain some inkling of
the economic realities of labour. Direct engagement
with the school curriculum, through school and house
councils, helps young teenagers, not just by allowing them
to have a voice but by encouraging them to follow things
through and take some responsibility for action. Schools
are modelled by adults, yet pupils have a distinctive and

sometimes revealing perspective. I was impressed by the serious purpose of teenagers in a West Midlands comprehensive to whom had been directly devolved part of the procedure for the appointment of new teachers. Given responsibility, most teenagers will step up, but there always need to be contingency plans to deal with the consequences when they do not.

Teenagers, just as much as adults, respond well when motivated. One key to motivation is being able to exercise some control over their school curriculum: being flexible about subject choice and as bespoke as possible with co-curricular activities helps to engage teenagers in choice and in accepting the consequence of their choice. For logistical reasons and through habit, schools tend to be wedded to formal lessons, but most pupils will remember best and treasure apparently unscripted social moments with adults. As a full boarding school, Eton is fortunate in arranging for all pupils to see their tutors in small groups in the evening. These tutorials take place in the tutor's home. Tutors are given guidance on issues to cover, supporting material and practical advice, and the general expectation is that most of the sex, drugs and rock 'n' roll issues will be discussed in the small-group setting. This can work extremely well. Teenagers feel respected and trusted to give their views. It takes skill from the teacher and some will feel inadequate to the task. Some, indeed, will argue that they became a teacher to teach chemistry or history, not this PSHE stuff. Yet it seems to be central to the role of a skilled teacher that they should be able to connect with issues that really matter to teenagers. This is an area where the training of teachers has been deficient.

Mental health

The more teachers are attuned to their pupils' social and health issues, the more help they can be in helping to identify problems. In my working lifetime, schools have been poor in identifying and dealing with mental illness, a deficiency born of ignorance, rather than intent. Only recently has mental health become a significant issue. While there is a great deal to be said for the old-fashioned premise that regular physical activity soothes the mind, that *mens sana in corpore sano*, a new appreciation of what makes for good mental health is overdue. With a better understanding of health, schools are better able to help with problems during troubled times.

And problems abound. Sitting in the head's seat offers a privileged, wide-angled view. There are more teenage mental health problems than parents might believe or wish to believe. The situation has got worse. It is tempting to interpret the high number of reported cases of mental illness as reflecting greater awareness and willingness to seek help, but there is no doubt that the pressures on teenagers have been mounting. It takes the form of peer pressure, especially via social media, pressure from parents to deliver, pressure from school to get good grades, and pressure from themselves to live up to the standards that the rest of the world has chosen. Given the potent cocktail of pressure handed to them, it is no surprise some teenagers buckle and can be deeply distressed. The problem is compounded because, in my experience, many parents do not understand what is going on and are worried, but they are fearful that admitting to difficulty will somehow be terminal for their child. There is only one way for parents to handle symptoms of distress: listen, do not disbelieve what you hear and be prepared to talk about it outside the family.

The symptoms can be deeply disturbing. An articulate, successful professional man tells me he cannot cope with his daughter's mood swings, at one moment happy, and then talking of suicide. He cannot, he confides, find any way to help her. In fact her behaviour is far from uncommon. Talk of depression and suicide is a well-documented feature of adolescent life, part of the process of experimenting with identity. If the talk of suicide is accompanied by a definite plan, then psychiatric help is urgently needed. If the talk is general, listen and be calm, do not be dismissive nor express frustration. A feature of the way adolescents react is their need to test adults to prove that they are useless (shades of Holden Caulfield in *The Catcher in the Rye*). An adolescent may well approach a situation assuming adults will be blunt and dismissive. Respond aggressively or unsympathetically and a parent may unwittingly play a part in a drama being enacted by their child.

Adults tend to create a climate in which young people feel adults cannot be spoken to. As with so many teenage issues, early regular open conversation about the things that matter to them in life helps enormously. And remember, do not try to be 'on their level'; be yourself and be consistent.

It is easy to advocate calm, steady reasonableness, altogether harder to practise it when you are worried sick about your child. I am conscious that there have been occasions when I have offered sage advice to parents and felt a bit of a fraud, because in many circumstances there are no ready solutions. Advice is a best guess based on experience and some knowledge, but understandably parents want to be told what to do. This is particularly true in cases of depression, for which parents need an ocean of patience. A temptation to tell a child to get on with it and make the most of his/her opportunity in school can be strong, but it is wholly unproductive. Many teenagers have times when a mood swing takes them low and they can work their way out of it by talking things through and being busy. The medical condition of depression, however, can be very deep and difficult. In these cases, experience shows that a quick resort to medication is the wrong route, not least because there are attendant dangers with anti-depressants. Medication can lift the mood for a while, but more lasting changes will come about in a regulated way with therapy and support.

One of the most testing times for a head is dealing with copycat events. A 16-year-old boy is harming himself by cutting his arms repeatedly. It transpires that he has a relationship with a boy in another school who is harming himself: though the 16-year-old would not see it as such, this is copycat behaviour. While not confined to the young, this kind of behaviour is marked in the teenage years and offers an interesting insight to the way teenagers can see the world.

Teenagers are more susceptible because their identities are shifting and changing; they are malleable. There is, perhaps, an element of novelty in aping extreme behaviour, but more telling is the propensity of teenagers, both boys and girls, to be attuned to negative signals to which they can adjust in ways that seem odd or out of proportion to adults. For both sexes, frontal lobe activity drives this reaction, sometime acutely so. Girls around the age of 14 tend to ruminate at length about their behaviour and seem over-sensitive to criticism. Breaking a cycle of copycat behaviour can be challenging. Sometimes it can be dealt with by removing the iconic figure, which allows others in the group the freedom to revert to their old selves.

At other times, the situation seems intractable. One school faced a series of teenage suicides spread over months. In a macabre way it seemed to be fashionable: it had become a kind of focused hysteria. The pressure on the school staff and families was intense. Steady work by chaplains and counsellors helped, together with clear leadership of the community, staying positive and communicating the benefits of positive behaviour. Often teenagers cannot see a clear way ahead and in a fuzzy world it is tempting to see the dark side, which can appear almost comforting. Adolescents need to experience a range of emotions and test their limits – sometimes they go too far.

For most parents, worries will revolve around relationships, isolation and bullying. The dynamic of a group of teenagers is fascinating to observe. Parents seldom see this: it is not something passed down in a parent's manual, but it is instructive. Pastoral figures in schools see teenage groups in action and those in the boarding-school world see a great deal. Teenage groups intuitively engage in role-playing: the group will have its alpha leader, its pacifier, joker, even its recessive (the 'persecuted' one). These roles can be changed and swapped over time. This is not a conscious or contrived process, but it happens and it happens for a purpose. Teenage groups need opposites, real differences, not bland neutrality. This is how teenagers learn to navigate complex relationships in adult life. A healthy group will have ebb and flow and will not exploit difference negatively; an unhealthy group becomes static and locked in stereotypes; a dysfunctional group will have too many of the same type. Some of the best pastoral work I have seen has been from a teacher talking to a whole group about their behaviour as a group. One bunch of 14-year-old boys, for example, had a wholly negative pattern of behaviour (endless backbiting) but, unusually, was stable: they had learnt to live that way and get by. When this behaviour was pointed out to them and discussed, they stopped and found a healthier, stable way.

Bullying behaviour can be dealt with through the group. Children generally read bullying very well. It is knowing how to deal with it that poses problems. Most schools have very clear guidelines about what to do and whom to see when in trouble, and these are important, but the issue underlying the majority of cases I have encountered has been self-esteem, both for the perpetrator and the victim. When I address parents at the outset of their child's school career, I say that our prime, shared objective is to enable each boy to be himself and that this is not always an easy task. Through the vicissitudes of adolescence, when identity is a slippery thing, it is challenging for a young teenager to know who he or she is, to feel comfortable about it and have the confidence to be it. Parents underestimate how tough it can be. In this climate, it is easy to see how bullying can flourish, as adolescents jockey for position in the group and test the limits of their boundaries.

Bullying is repeated behaviour by a person who uses strength or influence to harm or intimidate those who are weaker. It basks in the sunlight of adulation: the perpetrator is cool, strong and may be feared, but is admired. In most cases, bullying stops when the audience is not impressed.

Conversations with 16-year-olds can reveal their amazement at patterns of their own behaviour a year or two previously. In short, most people grow out of a bullying and bullied phase. This realization makes the actual experience no easier to bear, and at times it can feel deeply painful and permanent, but good work in schools with individuals and especially with groups helps young people understand what they are doing. And relationships do change over time. More than once I have seen a group of 14-year-olds exhibiting vicious behaviour with others turn into a group of 18-year-olds who choose happily to go on holiday together. Bully and victim can become good friends.

As with so much with the life of an adolescent, there are few fixed points. It is like the ultimate fairground experience, a rollercoaster ride with the distortion of a hall of mirrors all in one. The bewildering, sometimes frightening path they tread is, at the same time, exciting and liberating: it is also necessary in order for them to grow into well-balanced, healthy adults. The one unchanging, vital, fixed point, the lodestar, is you, the parent – resolute in love whatever comes your way.

6

Character and Discipline

Character education has become fashionable again. Politicians and social commentators perceive imbalance in our current approach to school education. It is as though there has been a slow realization that the great stress placed on improvement of academic performance has distorted our inherited traditional belief that schools should help fashion morally aware people who make good citizens. The quest is on to find a fresh voice for character education.

The recently established Jubilee Centre for Character and Virtues, part of the school of education at the University of Birmingham, is a new and serious attempt to create shape around an area that can seem formless or, at least, difficult to pin down. The phrase 'character education' is a loose umbrella term covering wide-ranging attributes, from being moral, well-mannered and civically minded to traditional, socially acceptable and compliant.

Seeking to understand character has been a human occupation for thousands of years and upholding some ideal of character education is as old as education itself. Yet somehow, even today, society's understanding of character is elusive. We cannot agree how to develop it in a way that is seen as broadly beneficial. Our growing sophistication and knowledge of techniques and technologies to develop the mind is not matched by our appreciation of how to deal with character.

While there are character programmes aplenty around the world, the Jubilee Centre is unique in the UK in its focus and approach. Its significance is that it is a research-based organization conducting projects in a wide range of state, faith and independent schools seeking to find a benchmark, a kind of modern common denominator. Its central enterprise, generating useful knowledge 'about how to foster good character in every area of our personal and public lives', is noble and potentially valuable, but it is also very tricky. The centre states its belief that character strengths 'are critical to human flourishing, can be exercised within all human contexts and are educable'. There are assumptions within this statement of intent, not least that character can really be taught, but the difficulty runs deeper. The language of character education tends to be high-sounding and rhetorical: definitions of moral goodness or civic virtue are difficult to articulate and can mean different things to different people. One man's active participation in community affairs is another man's irritating busybody.

There are two attendant dangers: discussion can fall readily into the 'motherhood and apple pie' category, and the idea that children can learn character through a module bolted on to the school curriculum is tenuous. With regard to the language, progress will only be made if broad terms are backed up with specific practical examples. When it comes to the school curriculum, progress will only be made if we are able to shake off the mentality that effective education is principally delivered in isolated segments.

It has been a feature of my life as Head Master of Eton, particularly in recent years, that I have been asked to comment about 'character' in a variety of gatherings. I am swift to point out that Eton, like any other school, is a continuing work in progress and it is a constant and necessary challenge for us to find better ways to create a school environment in which young people feel that they are developing themselves, where they have space and opportunity but in which there is a kind of invisible mesh ensuring that no individual pupil is allowed to fall through. Yet I am conscious that a school like Eton enjoys three distinct advantages over most state schools: time, resources and tradition.

As a full boarding school, we have our pupils living in a community throughout the day and the week. We consciously shape our days to allow the time for boys to be engaged in a range of activity which develops in them the skills and habits that can nurture character. In addition, though the tide of bureaucracy has risen, our teachers are less constrained by box-ticking exercises. We have the resources, too: as a head I have been in the fortunate position of having both the financial and human capital upon which to draw to make our model of education work. When it comes to any attempt to devise a coherent approach to character education, having staff who 'get it' is crucial, and they are the more likely to develop this understanding when the traditions of the school feed them. It becomes a virtuous circle: when a school has the confidence born of experience to give time and resources to character education, the more confidence it breeds in teachers.

Writing in this broad-brush way runs the risk of succumbing to the generalities that characterize discussion about character education. So I suggest four things, each with a practical example, that might translate well into an altogether different school environment.

In the first place we should try to treat our teenagers as adults, with relationships based on trust. A recent relational teaching study by the International Boys' School Coalition has shown across the English-speaking world that boys' academic success is strongly influenced by the quality of relationship a student has with his teacher. One way Eton seeks to build relationships is to ensure that each boy has a tutor aside from the usual hierarchical school structure. Tutor groups number no more than six boys of the same age who come from a mix of boarding houses. Tutorials take place in the intimate surroundings of a teacher's home made possible because all teachers live in school accommodation within walking distance. Boys learn to talk and to listen; adults, too. The setting is easier to achieve given the particular advantages of a boarding school, but the key thing is giving priority to apparently informal, small-group discussions that encourage respectful peer relationships. I have seen something similar achieved with considerable effect in day schools. It is important to give tutorials of this kind priority within the curriculum and not simply tack them on as an afterthought or use them as an administration session for calling the register.

Second, young people flourish if they grow in a culture which offers them the opportunity to take a lead. The gurus of well-being see this approach as essential: pupils need to volunteer, to be given a degree of autonomy, to be creative and to run their own show. An Eton example is the tradition that visiting speakers are invited by the boys. In a typical year there will be over two hundred visiting speakers on all manner of subjects. All the arrangements, from travel, refreshments and venue, to the running of the event itself, often inviting students from other schools, are organized by the boys. It takes considerable effort and encouragement from teachers to enable pupils to fly solo, and there is always the risk that teenagers will get things wrong or let you down, but the confidence they gain is remarkable. The aim is to create a culture in which teenagers see it as *normal* to fix a meeting with a politician's office or speak to a leading academic or businessman on the phone. This approach has been modified and adopted successfully by some state day schools that we know. The key is giving teenagers the support to reach out confidently to the adult wold.

Third, students need to learn to deal with failure as well as success. When I go through the exercise of Taking Leave each year, where traditionally the Head Master sees each 18-year-old leaver individually, I find I am most concerned for the golden boy for whom everything has been too easy, even more than I am for the student who needs huge encouragement to participate. Schools need to create contexts from which pupils can learn lessons from failure. Eton believes in competition, be it for a higher sports team or teaching group which are selected on the basis of recent performance. In my experience, boys enjoy competition. It excites and encourages them. The challenge for us as teachers is to help them deal with the consequences of competition, and in particular, to appreciate the virtue of perseverance, bouncing back from a disappointment, sticking at things and seeing them through. There is no joy in seeing a teenager fail or be rejected, but it is folly to shield them from the rhythms of life, even if (particularly if) the parents are hovering in attendance, trying to write the script.

Fourth, ambition. I visit schools where the idea of personal ambition is frowned upon. It is seen to be an individualist's charter, the antithesis of good community living. Yet encouraging young people to have the ambition and confidence to try things and believe in the possible should be an essential tenet of every teacher's mission. I speak here of a true sense of self-worth, not the glib self-confidence that can tip into arrogance. With self-belief, I have hope that the students I see leaving school will be able to look after themselves and be useful to other people. To this end, parity of esteem within a school is crucial. Pupils need to feel valued for what they are and what they can do, so a boy who runs a social project is celebrated just as much as the star rugby player. Schools tend automatically to laud individual success or excellence, but the higher praise should go to the teenagers who take a lead and get things done. The best captain of a sports team may well not be the best player and that, too, is a lesson to learn.

There are many other examples, the list is extensive and perhaps that makes the point: there is no silver bullet to the development of character but a host of small ways, regularly and repeatedly given, that creates the context in which character education is likely to happen. In short, it is a matter of school culture: what everyone involved, teacher and pupil, feels is valued and expected. It is also a matter of creating the small communities within a school that reinforce the culture, whether it is the immediacy of boarding-house life or 'vertical' tutor groups or clubs and societies.

As a parent choosing a school, I would naturally enough be drawn to statistics and tables, but I would also wish to know how a school creates its sense of supportive community at every level and how it helps young people develop the character to be rounded and grounded, useful people, how it deals with success and failure. And I would ask for specific examples.

I would also wish to have a sense of what 'discipline' means.

Discipline

For A. C. Benson character did not merit a chapter. To Benson and his colleagues the education of character was self-evidently part and parcel of what a school did; indeed, it was the point of it. He was more concerned about the overweening prominence given to sports by society at large, as though character was exclusively formed on the football field. He was concerned, too, that intellectual life and academic performance did not enjoy sufficient prominence, for the development of the mind is also a matter of character. Yet Benson was quite clear about the significance of one essential element in this debate: discipline. 'The power to maintain discipline', he writes, 'is the *unum necessarium* for a teacher; if he has not got it and cannot acquire it, he had better sweep a crossing.'

Sound classroom discipline is the bottom line. Without it all the best intentions, initiatives and programmes flounder and sink. Most of us recognize the symptoms, the nervousness and increasing desperation of the teacher, while the young, who welcome a break from the rigour of learning and scent blood, push to the limits and beyond their own expectations of behaviour. We were most of us guilty as children. I recall the 13-year-old me with a group of reasonably intelligent boys tacitly arranging to subvert a new young teacher's seating plan by swapping places when he looked down into his book, thus enabling us with honesty to say we were not the person he called upon. Before long, a full-scale chess game had developed with more daring moves across the desks, like a knight, two up and one along. The young teacher's eyes became all the more firmly fixed on his book and for longer periods of time: we knew we had won. He lasted one term. Of the stress he felt we had no knowledge and no interest. We would have been amazed and upset to discover how wretched we had made him.

Not much changes. Benson quotes an example given by a friend from an unnamed public school around 1900:

the conversation was general, books were flying across the room, the whole class was used to rise to their feet every time the clock struck and made for the door with an air of blithe unconsciousness… the master left his seat too and hurried to the door to put his back against it.

One well-intentioned boy who was heard asking the others to behave succumbed within minutes of the next lesson and was 'busily employed in constructing a long rope of quill pens, which he pushed, as a sweep pushes his jointed brush, across the room to his friends opposite'.

The common difficulty of new young teachers is failing properly to cross the line from student to teacher. Wishing to be warm-hearted and generous, wishing to be consensual and not dictatorial and, too often, wishing to be more a friend than a professional, is the road to schoolroom chess and ropes of quill pens. All teachers new to the classroom need to know two things: that they must be tougher than they feel is intuitively right (it is always possible to lighten up with a class but very difficult to reinvent yourself as a disciplinarian), and that they should clearly outline parameters of behaviour stating what will be tolerated and what will not, and they should consistently stick to these rules.

There are other 'strategies' for the teacher, more common sense than tricks of the trade – knowing each pupil by name as soon as possible, for example (feeling anonymous fuels poor behaviour). Teachers must know their subject material well and admit ignorance if a bright spark asks an awkward question (and always remember to follow up the question at the next lesson). Teachers must own the space, too, being in the classroom before the pupils if at all possible. Sometimes some simple theatre helps; one head of department had the knack of calming the class of a teacher in difficulty by standing in the doorway of the teacher's room so that the pupils had to walk past the head of department into a space they felt she controlled; whatever the psychology, it worked. Respect for the teacher's room is an extension of respect for the teacher. Above all, a consistent and fair approach to pupils is what they respond to best. When it comes to 'winning over' a class, the pupils' knowledge that their teacher knows her stuff, is concerned about their achievement and will not back off or disappear, makes the prospect of playing up less appealing. Most young people in most schools want to gain something from the experience; they want to be won over.

This is not just true for the classroom, but for the school as a whole. It is a natural human predisposition to wish to be involved with something that feels good and is recognized by others as good; to be on a winning team. For all the talk of spirals of despair, there is a corresponding virtuous circle that lifts communities. It takes unrelenting hard work. However good an individual teacher may be, her job will be made very much harder if she works in a school in which there is not whole-hearted commitment to upholding a culture of respect, which is the bedrock of discipline. In the best boarding schools senior people such as house masters routinely walk the corridors and talk to pupils, conveying their expectations and standards informally through conversation. So, too, in day schools all levels of management need to be seen to be engaged in the daily lives of pupils. The most disastrous boarding houses I have known have been run by house masters who have hidden behind the green baize door of their study. One communicated with his charges by sticking post-it notes on pupils' bedroom doors: small wonder he was known as 'Mr Nobody'. A tale is told of times past at Eton when a green-baize-door house master found his house entirely deserted. His boys had decamped en masse to another house and emphatically made their point.

It is in the small moments and day-to-day conversations that culture and discipline are built: and this means listening to the young. At Eton I inherited an archaic tradition known as the Bill. If a boy breaks any kind of school rule, his house master is obliged to speak to the Head Master at the mid-morning break known as Chambers. The situation is outlined and a possible sanction discussed. The errant boy is then called to see the Head Master formally, usually just before lunch. The Head Master sees all boys from year 11 upwards, his deputy deals with the younger boys. The Bill takes place each working day, six days a week.

It is unusual to find a head teacher personally dealing with a wide range of disciplinary matters ranging from missing chapel or repeatedly being late for lessons to serious incidents that might merit expulsion. In truth, it has on occasion proved a chore and is certainly time-consuming. Younger masters query its usefulness; others should deal with pupils, they say, the head should spend more time on them. Yet it took me only a few weeks to appreciate that the Bill is no dead tradition but a vibrant and necessary point of focus in the day. I see each boy separately and ask him for his account of what has happened and on around one in five occasions there is more to the story than I had been told or had been apparent. I discuss the sanction with the boy and tell him there is no expectation on my part that he should necessarily agree with the action I am about to take, but I do expect him to understand why I have done it. The Bill is, in fact, a powerful opportunity to convey and discuss values that are at the heart of civilized behaviour. In particular, it provides an opportunity for teenagers seriously to consider what it means to take responsibility for their actions.

By tradition, the process is in the presence of a praeposter, a senior boy who stands at the back of the room and observes all. While I would never invite his comments in front of the billed boy, I have frequently found subsequent conversation illuminating and usually reassuring. That the punishment is meted out witnessed by another pupil has a strangely modern feel to it, a twist on 'pupil voice', an example perhaps of the resilience of the best traditions.

Some of my encounters in the Bill have been dramatic, such as the boy who hyperventilated in front of me, or comic, such as the boy who spent some considerable time fixing a sling for his bowing arm in order to get out of his cello lesson only to be seen miraculously healed as he left the lesson. Some have been difficult and truculent, such as the boy who prefaced each of our not infrequent Bill meetings with the formula, 'It wasn't my fault...' After leaving school he was jailed for some hair-brained scam, doubtless telling the judge, 'It wasn't my fault...' We failed with him. One or two have had something of the dark about them which has led to extensive conversations with parents. Most, however, are good boys who have slipped up and I would far rather have them learn some basic truths about dealing with people in the relatively safe context of a school.

The telling feature about the Bill with its formality and theatre is that it works on teenagers who want it to work. There is a kind of ritualistic dance about the exchange, but if the Head Master and boys know there is an element of game to be played, that is a lesson in itself. Boys take their punishment and move on, having learnt a little on the way. It is the boys who go 'beyond the Bill' who are likely to occupy a great deal of time and who will need an individual route out of the mess they are in.

Boys learn to stand or fall as a group. A bunch of friends caught together, for, say, indulging in an alcoholic party is likely to have differing levels of involvement and culpability. I always ask the boys if they would wish to go through the individual details or to be treated in the same way as part of the group: it is rare to find a group who will not elect to be treated as one, and that, too, is a lesson about friendship. A quiet boy on the fringes who accepts a communal punishment finds his reputation enhanced. There can be surprising benefits from a formal system of discipline and punishment, thoughtfully applied.

The Bill is a way for the Head to take the temperature of the school every day and also to keep an eye on his 25 house masters each of whom will have his own sometimes idiosyncratic take on discipline. The house master who never seems to have miscreants is as much a concern as the one who too frequently bills his boys.

The structure of the Bill, or its equivalent, offers a basic framework, but in itself has little intrinsic value. It is the spirit in which proceedings are undertaken that gives the business validity. A mechanical process, operating on a rigid template of sanctions, will soon be viewed as another irritating routine. Listening to pupils, trying to help them understand what they have done, gives what might be a sterile exercise some pastoral purpose.

That is the heart of it. Any good system of school discipline will establish parameters to enable everyone in the community to get on with their lives productively and will establish notions of right and wrong, but it should also enable young people, at a natural time of experimentation, to understand that there are always consequences to actions and the lives of other people are affected. Pupils need to feel that the system of discipline (and by extension the heart of the school) is in the right place. This means dealing with each case on its own merit and taking the context into account. In essence, it is about developing trust.

It was interesting to note that in an age when the young were not spared the rod A. C. Benson wrote, 'I am no believer in punishments: indeed, I think that a set punishment is merely a sign of weakness. Small punishments are simply irritating, and it is far better to give several warnings and then come down with all your might. Only deliberate offences deserve punishment.' As so often, Benson is near the mark. It is the repetition of the same offences, failing to learn from the experience, that merits a vigorous response. A modern system can readily discriminate between a first offence for a relatively minor issue, which is dealt with by automatic sanction (even delivered these days by email), and a repeated or serious matter which would lead to an appearance in front of the head.

I am sometimes asked how it is possible to run a full boarding school with 1,300 teenage males in the twenty-first century. The questioner may assume we run a tough regime of military precision. The truth is that the school operates well (indeed operates at all) because at root the pupils want it to work. They have to trust the school.

It would be very easy for everything to unravel. Large numbers of intelligent young men can make their feelings known very clearly. Early on in my time as Head, a small group of older boys felt that the testing for drugs on four of their fellows had not been properly executed. They rather brilliantly organized a protest of several hundred boys on the public street in front of the hall which held the usual mid-morning meeting, making a lot of noise until I addressed them and asked to speak with their chosen representatives, at which point the crowd dispersed. It became clear that the boys had a garbled and false view of what had happened with the drug-testing, but just as clearly there had not been sufficient trust. We needed to work on it, not least by being more direct in the way we communicated with boys.

There is a phrase of inherited Eton wisdom, variously attributed, that 'if you trust boys they will let you down, if you don't they will do you down'. At the time of the anti-Iraq war marches in London, two boys came to see me to ask permission to go along with a group of others. I listened to them, they were genuine in their commitment and I felt it right that they should be allowed, with their parents' permission, to attend. It was agreed that they would attend as individuals and not as representatives of the school. At the event they marched under a banner bearing the legend 'Eton College Orwell Society' and attracted considerable publicity. They had let me down. The subsequent incoming fire from some outraged correspondents was directed at me. Sometime later I discovered this militant group of boys had debated whether or not to ask permission at all, some feeling that it would be more of a statement simply to walk out of school and go. They took a vote which was in favour of asking for permission. On reflection, I was glad they went and with my blessing.

Trust is born of relationships nurtured day by day. A school master needs the resilience repeatedly to bounce back having been let down by the young, but experience also gives the school master confidence that teenagers learn and in the longer term will respond positively. One very good house master faced the ignominy of having to bill two-thirds of his house after an official Christmas party was extended unofficially into the small hours. Twelve months later a group of those same boys came to assure him that the event would pass smoothly and well, which it did: they had been embarrassed by the consequence for their house master and wished to make amends.

In a considerable majority of cases teenagers respond very well when they are clear in their minds what needs to be done. A house master who faced a domestic tragedy found his boys exceptionally well organized and disciplined during his difficult personal time. The wearing thing from the adult perspective is how frequently teenagers seem to misread situations or fail to predict an evident outcome, but that is the teenage condition. Teachers and parents need to understand this phase of human development and to ride with it, being clear about expectations, endlessly discussing the reasons why, and accepting teenagers for what they are. When it comes to developing the character of our teenagers, we need to be willing to trust and prepared to be let down.

7

Imagination

A vibrant imagination is not an 'outcome' that can be 'delivered', it is a quality that cannot be taught in a didactic way and it is not the content for a module, but it is the most important quality young people take into their later lives.

When Keats referred to the 'truth of the imagination' he acknowledged that it is through the imagination that we create a moving landscape in which the different contours and shapes of all the impressions and images around us begin to form a coherent picture. In that sense, imagination is the truth of what we see and hear. Great teaching stimulates imagination.

It is the imagination that allows us not just to feel unthreatened by the vast landscape and distant horizon that lie before us, but to celebrate the unknown beyond the horizon. As the poet David Whyte observes, it is through the imagination that we learn the crucial lesson as a child that the world exists without us and that, rather than being frightened by that revelation, we can begin to embrace life at the limits and beyond the limits of our understanding.

As a consequence, it is imagination that gives us the flexibility and lightness of mind to respond to all that life has to offer, a resilience more profound than anything achieved through intellectual or physical discipline.

Teachers are faced with a dilemma. A good teacher will take a child's imagination to the edge, beyond the boundaries of the comfortably known world to new frontiers, and will present the world afresh each day knowing that it is by addressing the unknown that true learning happens. Yet school systems tend to see the classroom experience as training, a means to place parameters around a child's freewheeling imagination and to teach useful skills and knowledge for adulthood. Sir Ken Robinson has memorably described the function of schooling as training the mind at the expense of the whole person with the aim of producing a tribe of university professors – a self-perpetuating circle of limitation. Meaningful education goes beyond training. That is the dilemma; teachers are judged professionally on measurable outcomes, yet most intuitively know that their role embraces more than this.

With a clarity and vehemence to match Illich, it is possible to condemn exam-obsessed British schools as counter-productive, lop-sided institutions merely fuelling the basic requirements of a capitalist economy. It is true that our largely Victorian process of examining acts as a break on creativity, that our rigid inspection regimes reduce evaluation to a lowest common denominator, but the situation is more complex. Despite apparent attempts to become more systematic (and thereby ape mechanical Chinese methods), the culture of teaching in Britain still has flexibility and resilience.

The key is not so much what is taught as the way it is taught. Arguments about choice of academic discipline and the balance of the curriculum tend to miss the point. Should the history syllabus teach our island story or the American Civil Rights Movement or the effects of colonialism? Should Religious Studies focus on the Gospels or on alternative religion or on feminist theology? Does English Literature mean the canon of Dead White European Males or the idioms of the street? The answer to all of these questions is all of the above.

Time dictates that choices must be made about the topics to be studied, but that in itself presents no barrier: it is the way the young are inspired that is critical. I have seen more energy, perception and personal engagement from a group of 16-year-olds discussing the Arab–Israeli conflict, with each pupil taking the lead on a different aspect, than I ever recall from the traditional lecture style of my own school days. I was passionate about history, yet my most vivid schoolboy recollection is not what I was told by a teacher but being asked to give a lecture to a group of some 40 of my peers, an experience beyond the syllabus which gave me my first thrill of something akin to teaching.

This is not just fertile ground for the humanities; an approach to maths that embraces problem-solving, collaborative work on an engineering project or a design initiative are all avenues to bringing learning alive, making the world afresh each day.

One recent positive development is the move towards 'linearity' at A Level. The changes to A Level introduced in 2000 brought in a modular approach. The intention was to relieve the pressure on pupils who previously had to take their hugely important A Level exams in one sitting. For many teachers the old regime had seemed a high-stakes approach with some students stumbling badly. There were advantages to a modular approach: it encouraged lower-sixth-formers to stay focused with their AS Level exams at the end of the first sixth-form year, and it suited some topic-based subjects, like maths, well; it also allowed some greater flexibility of choice when students came to select their principal subjects at the end of the lower sixth, having had the experience of the halfway house of AS Level exams. Given the facility to retake modules repeatedly, it was also seen as a means to achieve and award higher grades. The problem, however, has been that in many subjects the modular approach stifles creativity.

Modern linguists were aghast to discover that their modular A Level syllabus was to concentrate on language skills to the exclusion of almost all cultural reference. Learning a language is, in any event, at the other end from maths on the modularity/linearity scale. It makes little sense to divide a cumulative skill into segments. To have reference to literature, media and society largely removed from the experience of language learning leaves the experience bare and mechanical. Science teachers who moved back from modularity to a linear syllabus surprised themselves at the benefits. Students had a better understanding and a more thorough grounding; more especially, they could make connections between themes and topics. Teachers felt liberated, enjoying their subject in a way that they had forgotten, feeling that they had the time to explore byways as well as take the highway, conveying real enthusiasm to their pupils.

In 2008, at the height of the modularity boom, the Cambridge Pre-U was launched as an alternative route to A Level. Pre-U courses were linear and attractive to universities because they offered finer grading of students' performance, but their strength was bringing breadth to the subject. An educated mind makes connections between phenomena; an imagination fired by the prospect of an expanding horizon engenders passion and enquiry.

The linearity/modularity issue in the sixth form is just one illustration of the significance of the way we teach and learn. The difference between syllabuses in the content of, say, a biology course may not be much different, but the approach to the content leads to a different experience.

In a similar way, our approach to the curriculum, where we are seen to place priority, affects our children's experience. In order to compete in a globalized economy, the current orthodoxy asserts the primacy of the STEM subjects: science, technology, engineering and mathematics. A comparison of statistics reveals just how far ahead some other countries are in preparation of their students for the technological world, particularly in the Far East. It makes sense to encourage more of our young people to commit to these relatively hard disciplines; good sense, too, to raise the general level of technological literacy; but we stand to lose a great deal by seeming to undervalue the arts. The exclusion of the arts from the English Baccalaureate (EBacc) for 16-year-olds, for example, is a mistake.

Engagement in music, art, drama and other arts is an essential part of the way our imagination develops. It is not the only route (as we have seen, every subject well taught pushes the learner's imagination towards a new frontier), but it offers a very particular way to appreciate better the fullness of the human condition. Art is a crucible in which man's manifold experiences mix together to produce something new and exciting. We trace man's desire to express himself through art from the very beginnings of human society; the instinct to art is a resonant human trait. Young people experiment with their own identities as part of growing up, and being invited by their teachers to explore themselves through the medium of art is essential. This is not a New Age fad: art helps create more rounded, rooted people who are able truly to see the world around them. Ironically, they are likely to be more effective in a globalized market place than those who have been fed on a simple diet of STEM.

I am often asked how Eton has changed since my school days in the late 1960s. Boys are more aware that it is a competitive and meritocratic world which they will have to navigate, and most work harder than used to be the case. In line with shifting social attitudes among the young, it is generally a kinder place, too. Yet what strikes me most is the seriousness with which the arts are taken. Academic distinction and success on the sports field are still highly regarded, but it is commitment to the cultural life of the school which is remarkably different. Whether on or behind stage, in any number of configurations of musical groups, experimenting with different artistic media, boys enjoy the arts and though they are unlikely to put it into words, they sense their value. It is still too often the case, however, that parents will cajole their sons into a choice of subjects less 'subjective' and more 'useful' and away from the arts. The arts matter deeply in school education, but there is a huge task to educate parents, some university tutors and, indeed, government to take the arts seriously.

Part of the problem lies in the attitude of schools. Putting on a school play or a major concert is valuable in itself, but is not a programme for the arts. In some schools it is hard to escape the feeling that culture-as-showcase is the point and purpose of the thing, more PR than reaching to the deep themes of our shared humanity. Indeed, there can be a danger in the pursuit of perfection, with a play, for example, being manicured and polished to such a degree that the life is squeezed out of it. Heads will want their young people to strive for excellence and aspire to be the best they can be on the public stage but the art of discovery is as important as the performance and pupils and teachers need reassurance that this is the case.

We want our young people to be adventurous explorers. A new world of fast-developing technologies is opening up fresh terrain for discovery. One reason exploring this new terrain is exciting is because there is a growing recognition that the 'infrastructure' subjects like science, technology, engineering and maths can be taken to a new dimension by imagination expressed through the creative arts: STEM becomes STEAM. Rather than just efficiently replicating the skills of the last generation, computer technologies are opening new frontiers. In school terms this means exploring the relationship between established silos of knowledge. As well as rehearsing the well-thumbed syllabuses of chemistry and physics, for example, school pupils will be creatively engaged exploring the area *between* them. It involves taking new knowledge and using it in a different way. Intellectual sparks will light fires in unexpected places and it will need adaptable, confident teachers to cope with the energy that is released.

Today's students will grow up to work in a world in which machines will be able to perform many of the functions of the professional middle classes, the kind of careers to which many young people now aspire. Machines will be able to diagnose illness and prescribe drugs, machines will be able to analyse situations and dispense legal advice; doctors and lawyers as we have come to know them may disappear, certainly their numbers could be dramatically reduced. It will be human imagination that will create these machines and human imagination that will ensure machines will operate within a human context.

Perhaps without realizing it, schools are already beginning to prepare their students for this change. The information young people need used to be found principally in books in the library or in the teacher's head. Today pupils walk around with the library of Alexandria in their pocket, encapsulated in a slender box of immense power, their smart phone. It is an unvetted library without a librarian which has tremendous potential to enable students to cross boundaries and explore new lands, but also the capacity to confuse and intimidate. The teacher's role increasingly will be to help pupils navigate this terrain, to make critical judgements about sources of information; in short, to discriminate.

New systems will offer help finding ways to develop the art of discrimination; indeed, identifying appropriate information for a particular purpose will be a growth area in computer technology. From a teenager's point of view, students will need to learn how to discriminate between the discriminators.

This sounds a brave new world, but the principles are as old as education. In the mid-nineteenth century the Eton schoolmaster William Cory claimed a great school was about learning 'the art of discrimination'. His ideas would not be out of place in Plato's *Republic*.

From time to time parents and teachers will be concerned about a particular pupil who seems obsessed with his computer, usually through a surfeit of gaming. Extreme cases are worrying and can require specialist help because it is a form of addiction. Experience suggests, however, that those who succumb are likely to have an addictive personality and to be susceptible to other types of addiction; the problem runs deep. In most cases of concern, the response should be light, a touch on the tiller. I would not be exercised by my child's preference for the computer screen if other aspects of her, or more likely, his life are in balance: that they socialize well, their school work is done on time, that they take exercise. In short, there is nothing inherently wrong with gaming, indeed, it can be a thoroughly good thing. The skills required, the speed and flexibility of thought and the stimulus to imagination, all indicate a worthwhile educational activity. If a child takes pleasure and benefit from half an hour or an hour's gaming online after school in the evening, this should offer no cause for alarm. As part of a balanced programme, it is healthy. It is a form of constructive play.

Finding time for constructive play is as important for teenagers as it is for younger children. Most people see virtue in play for the very young. Play takes many forms from shaking a rattle to hide and seek and can be a solo activity or as part of a group. The National Literacy Trust identifies 10 reasons why play is important, including laying the foundation for literacy by performing new sounds, trying out vocabulary and storytelling. Play also promotes learning new skills, being spontaneous, making decisions, practising physical movement. Crucially, the NLT observes that a prime function of play is giving adults the chance to learn to play again, encouraging adults to communicate with their children at a profound level, refreshing the ability to be contented and sociable. Play is good for all ages. Yet schools seem frightened of it, either creating an intimidating bustle of activity or urging pupils to be off the school premises as soon as possible: broadly speaking, the former will be the mark of a good school, the latter of an inadequate one. But both approaches miss something important.

If school pupils are able to see constructive play as an integral part of school life and not as an antidote to routine and pressure to be found only outside school, attitudes and atmosphere can change dramatically. I have felt and seen the contrast when visiting two similar schools facing similar challenges and serving similar housing estates: in one, life seemed a drudgery, counting the minutes to the end of the school day, in the other there was anticipation of the next school event. In the latter, time was given to pupils to enable them to socialize in comfortable, bright areas where creative activities were encouraged; it was a school in which, for example, all students would have the opportunity to play a musical instrument, and they did. Not surprisingly, measurable learning 'outcomes' were higher in this purposely relaxed culture than in a school going through the motions.

A problem for heads has been the growth of demands on school time, the sheer volume of curriculum stuff, whether EBacc, testing, courses ending with the suffix-ship (citizenship, leadership etc.), British values and so on. As an independent school head I have been protected from many of these demands, but state school colleagues tell me that the noises have become a tumult; they wish for a little peace and quiet to get on with the business of education. Small wonder that feeling such pressure on time, schools will shy away from allowing apparently unproductive opportunities for play.

The traditional boarding-school model has always seen timetabled time just as one part of the whole. Lessons have specific slots in the day, but whole afternoons can be given over to other activities where arrangements are looser and which will not involve all pupils at the same time. Pupils will have fallow periods when they are expected to organize themselves, time for meeting friends, playing a game of kick-about football, catching up on some music practice or even a spot of gaming – and all this done in school time. In this way a school more readily reflects the rhythms of life. It goes without saying that pupils will sometimes abuse the trust placed in them to use time well, but as the saying has it, it is the job description of a teenager to let adults down. The benefits of self-discovery, downtime and simply having fun, all of which are part of healthy growth and thriving imaginations, outweigh the occasional problem.

This is self-evidently harder to achieve in a day school with more limited time, but I have seen it done. On the surface this might seem a philosophy of less is more, less directed time leads to more engagement and better results, but I see it differently. More time directed by pupils and more trust leads to a better education.

Originality

A.C. Benson expresses his concern about the life of the imagination through his observations about 'originality'. His principal concern seems to be to defend the public school system circa 1900 against the charge that, being built upon conventions, 'it is a foe to all originality'. He asserts that 'the only originality that is worth having is that of the mind and the heart, and I doubt whether that is ever extinguished by superficial conventionalities' and goes on to claim that 'questions of dress and deportment become simply mechanical and habitual and leave the mind free to concern itself with other matters'. There is some truth in this observation. School uniform is sometimes criticized as a suppression of individuality, but the reverse is true. By removing distinctions in dress – a form of difference that is often a consequence of family wealth – and by insisting on some general rules of appearance – hair length and so on – some of the outward superficial differences between young people are reduced. Attention is more likely then to focus on character and ability: what young people say and do rather than what they wear.

Eton is a school more outwardly conventional than most, and does indeed feed off its traditions. School dress, which for boys is a tailcoat, waistcoat and striped trousers, with something very similar for masters, is an anachronism. To the public eye a parade of penguins on a public street between lessons is an extraordinary sight. It was once the case that I had occasion to sit next to a leading fashion guru at an event at Eton. I was wearing school dress which she described as 'radical chic': this, it has to be said, was an unusual reaction. Yet there is something about the strangeness of the dress that is both embracing and protective. Whatever a boy's family background, be it tower block or castle, once dressed in its antique garb, he belongs. By virtue of being dressed identically, boys value each other for something deeper than appearance.

So it is with routines. A traditional boarding school has many rules and restrictions. The whereabouts of pupils need to be known throughout the day and at certain times they will have to sign out and to be accountable for their movements. They do not have the ease of access to some of the activities other teenagers might enjoy. Yet it is a notable feature of life at Eton that a boy recognizes that it is through respecting the basic rules of the place, playing the game, that considerable freedom and possibility open up to him. Boys trusted on the basics of school life are given considerable licence to follow their own interests and enthusiasm. It is a great lesson for life: embrace routine and it will free you.

The relationship between rules and routines on the one hand and freedom of imagination on the other is frequently misunderstood. Schools that are liberal in the sense that anything goes, actually limit their pupils' choices and imaginations.

Benson has two further interesting points to make about 'originality'. The first concerns sport. The overwhelming dominance of sport in Edwardian public schools he sees as a singular threat to the development of intellect and imagination. He acknowledges both the contemporary public 'wave of feeling' in favour of athletic endeavour and the capacity of great civilizations to be healthy both in body and in mind. Yet he expresses concern about the 'deadening effect of a solid diet of sport which makes young people apt to lose balance and proportion of mind and life altogether'.

In an age when school playing fields have been sold off and sporting bodies struggle to increase participation rates, despite the popular success of events such as the Olympics, such comments may well seem locked in another age. I would be among the first to extol the virtues of sporting education in terms of personal development and teamwork, learning to cope with victory and defeat, and yet there is an underlying truth. The teenager obsessed with sport, to the exclusion of other activity, may be physically healthier than the teenager obsessed with computers, but the effect is the same: be it games or gaming, obsession limits the imagination and stunts growth.

The second point concerns teachers. When I read fiction about school life from Benson's time, I sense space. There seems room to breathe. Unfettered by exam and inspection regimes, pupils and teachers are able to follow their own paths. Even at the time of writing I suspect it was a romantic view, but the contrast with our regulated age is sharp. We can seem busy for the sake of being busy. Yet even in what may have been a less pressured age, Benson acknowledges that constraints of time prove damaging to the teacher's own well-being. A vocationally driven teacher, in particular, is one who may suffer. Teachers all too readily spin along like busy tops, convincing themselves that they have done their duty, but there can be little nourishment along the way and problems can be considered too hastily and scantily. Prompt action seems better than quiet reflection and most teachers have 'time to do the one, and no time at all to do the other'.

Lack of time to reflect and recharge is a regular refrain from teachers. Many outside the teaching world find this hard to believe and are unsympathetic. Teachers have enormously long holidays, up to 16 weeks in the year, and it seems incredible that they can even contemplate moaning about their lot. While it is hard to argue with the bare facts, the difference is in the intensity of their work and its effect on personal life, particularly family life. There are few jobs in which there is such public scrutiny. Lesson observation may be one thing, but the scrutiny is more immediate and more demanding from the pupils in every class a teacher takes. A teacher cannot have an off day and reschedule the workload. He or she operates in the here and now and a classroom can be an exposed and unforgiving place for someone underprepared or under pressure. There is a great deal of giving, drawing from a personal well of knowledge, experience and skill, until it can run dangerously dry. Most teachers will collapse in an exhausted heap at the end of the term, but the dedicated will replenish their stock in holiday time. Even that replenishment may not be sufficient. A teacher's imagination needs to be as fresh and vigorous as their pupils. This is not an issue that has ever really been taken seriously in British schools.

A small number of British schools will offer a paid sabbatical to teachers during the course of their career at the school. This is small beer by comparison with some schools in Australia and America where paid leave of absence specifically to restore, develop and extend teachers' repertoire and enthusiasm is regularly given and is seen as money well spent. It is not just a question of extended time away from school. Professional development programmes offer more training opportunities and, in many cases, make money for them more readily available than in the past. Training about professional technique is well and good, but there needs to be similar weight given to teachers' subject knowledge, to their ability as communicators and their own sense of personal progression. Helping to fund a PhD, for example, or a course to enhance skills in a second language, or to match the curiosity of a teacher who wishes to find out more about a topic tangentially related to her subject: all these are ways to give practical help. For a school, wishing to be seen offering these opportunities is in itself an important statement of intent. Such a school values the life of the imagination in all members of its community.

8

Spirituality

It is a gloomy weekday morning. Gloom hangs above the heads of the black-coated rows of boys in chapel; disconnected minds roam somewhere, anywhere other than where they are. Suddenly there is a break in the clouds and sunlight casts sharp splashes of colour on the stone wall. Everyone raises their heads as one, the light dances. For a moment we are beyond ourselves, taken out of the here and now together.

There are scientific explanations for the effect of sunlight on stained glass, as there are for spectacular cloud formations or the threatening intimacy of the sea, yet there is some part of us that responds in a way beyond reason, aware of our smallness and perhaps seeing some higher purpose. Young children react spontaneously and with an open mind to different and unusual situations. A child kneels unprompted just because a place feels special, or asks if a disembodied voice in a cavernous space is the voice of God, or gives personalities to features of the natural world. Children respond intuitively to what they experience; they feel and freely express wonder.

The word 'spirituality' suggests some kind of transforming experience. The word itself has undergone several transformations, wrenched from its religious heritage to become a loose hold-all for any activity that might seem meaningful. For me the defining quality of spiritual life is wonder. It is the capacity to experience, accept and take joy in things beyond our understanding. In an instinctive way children are open to wonder. Through the teenage years we do our best to teach wonder out of them.

A glance at the guidelines for inspection of schools is revealing. Unlike inspection regimes in other parts of the world, in the UK there has been an attempt to embrace the spiritual, moral, social and cultural dimension of growing up. It is a difficult area to assess, however, and given the propensity to measure as much of school life as possible, these dimensions of school life often feel like a postscript to the real business of identifying a school's quality. In times past words like 'awe' and 'wonder' have appeared in the inspection rubric, but they seem quietly to have been shelved as though too difficult and flaky a concept. And in any event, if the results are good, the stats spot on, who is going to quibble about the quality of spiritual life, whatever that is?

As if in recognition of the difficulty, the four dimensions of spiritual, moral, social and cultural life have been lumped together, creating a superstore of soft values reduced to the acronym SMSC. Each dimension can have an impact on the others, but they are not interchangeable.

The language of the SMSC monolith has a strong civic tone. Schools should 'suitably prepare students for life'; all pupils 'should grow and flourish, become confident individuals and appreciate their own worth and that of others'. That is a sound basis for citizenship; indeed, a true sense of self-worth is the necessary condition to become a good citizen.

Yet the rubric about spiritual development seems to be an extension of the same idea. Spiritual development, we are told, is demonstrated by 'young people's beliefs which inform their perspective on life, their interest in and respect for other values, their enjoyment and fascination in learning, their use of imagination and creativity and their willingness to reflect on their experiences'. All these are qualities devoutly to be wished for because they augment the quality of our lives, yet there is little sense of reaching beyond everyday experience. The mention of fascination and imagination points somewhere in the direction of a life beyond the self, but there is no reference to wonder.

No wonder then that a teenager's capacity to taste the fullness of human experience is constrained. Many parents and teachers wish to broaden their children's horizons so that they can understand the contours of the landscape as far as they can see and also have a sense that there is something beyond the horizon. Schools tend to be good at helping pupils recognize and analyse points in the landscape, rather less good at enabling young people to have breadth of vision. The parts tend to have more significance than the whole. For practical and historical reasons schools tend to operate through discrete departments and areas, and there tends to be relatively little that is joined-up in the way schools think about what the pupils experience (indeed, I have seen different departments approach the same topic in contradictory ways). A culture of measuring the measurable has exerted a further downward pressure on schools to focus on the detail of a child's experience, sometimes at the expense of seeing the child as a whole person. The problem with a box-ticking mentality is not so much the ticking as the impulse to build more boxes.

We should not give up on wonder. In his book *The Magic of Reality*, aimed at school-age readers, Richard Dawkins elegantly explains the wonders of nature in scientific terms, from rainbows to DNA. He tackles questions like 'Why do we have night and day?' and 'Who was the first person?' He debunks notions that were once mythological or fabulous through the steady explanation of science, serving to show that the 'real' world of the scientifically provable is magical and wonderful. Yet this approach seems constrained and limited, a tad too measured, like fitting the world into boxes.

Accepting that there are aspects of life beyond the provable is a way to become a full human being. Hamlet tells his more prosaic friend, 'There are more things in heaven and earth, Horatio,/ Than are dreamt of in your philosophy.'

St John beautifully expresses the free-flowing nature of spiritual life in the words, 'The wind bloweth where it listeth, and thou hearest the sound thereof, but canst not tell whence it cometh, and whither it goeth: so is every one that is born of the Spirit' (John 3:8, AV). This is not the stuff to be found in a targeted school curriculum. Rather, it comes from an attitude of mind and an openness of heart, a willingness to open up the senses and not shut them down.

This attitude of mind and openness of heart comes from a habit of enquiry. The glory of human endeavour is the capacity to search for understanding and the perseverance to see things through. Perseverance, that most unromantic of virtues, is closely allied to wonder. We can experience a moment of wonder as a fleeting thing, like the splash of colours reflected from a stained-glass window, but it comes more profoundly when our searching reveals some truth or better understanding, that moment when at last a problem or an issue makes sense and in doing so reveals that there are more doors to be opened, leading to the prospect of further unknown possibilities. It is a moment that is at the same time rewarding and disconcerting.

In a sermon, Bishop Kallistos Ware, an English bishop in the Eastern Orthodox Church, refers to early Christians who captured this idea in a passage that did not find its way into the Gospels; 'Let him who seeks not cease from seeking until he find; and when he finds he will be troubled, and when he has been troubled he may be filled with wonder.' I have seen wonder like this in a classroom and in the wider life of the school, when a child realizes that the narrow horizon drawn by immediate pressures and interests is suddenly lifted to embrace a new world. And this is by no means confined to Religious Studies lessons; I have seen it in literature when a character's motivation and its implications become clear; in geography, when the scale of the natural world and the awful consequences of man's impact on the environment become apparent; in physics, when the boundaries of the universe shift and the miracle of existence on a tiny planet comes into focus; indeed, in every area of the curriculum. It takes good teaching to bring a child to the point of discovery and it is an extraordinary thing to witness. It is wonderful.

A secondary element in my definition of the spirit is belonging. Schools are hard-pressed by the many demands made on them, demands which drive them deeper into an accountable, material world. Challenging though it can be, schools need to make the time to create the opportunities for pupils to experience the spirit, and one significant way to do this is to celebrate being together.

Connecting with other human beings is a natural human desire; connecting with people beyond the family is a way of expressing personal identity: these are valuable social interactions. But connecting to a broader group, subsuming personality and momentary worries and desires into something far greater can have a spiritual dimension. Witness the intensity of silence in an act of collective worship or the intensity of noise at a rock festival.

Being part of a crowd with common purpose allows the burden of identity to be parked for a while and some common sentiment to be shared. As history shows us, this may not necessarily be a benign experience, as loss of self-awareness is not the same as elevation of the spirit, but it is the sense of belonging that drives people to repeat the experience.

A sense of belonging is of huge significance to teenagers. It may sound as though it is pushing it to claim that being in a netball or rugby team is a spiritual experience, but observing many teenagers over the years, there is some truth in it. Teenagers' quest for personal identity is shaped by their experience of collective identity. It is a natural process for a 14-year-old to want to be as much like the others in a group as possible and, a few years later, to feel able to be different. With growing maturity comes a developing critical faculty and the peer group is no longer the most significant point of reference. It is fascinating to see teenagers grow into an awareness of choice – that it is possible to be a self-directing, autonomous individual with all the opportunities and responsibilities that brings – and at the same time to choose to be part of a larger group. Fascinating, too, to see them become critical of group behaviour. They learn to understand the benefits and virtues of a commonwealth, giving over some personal freedoms for a greater, collective good.

If an aim of education in school is to develop critically aware young people who evolve an ability to navigate group dynamics, how then can schools justify obliging their pupils to do certain things, attending lessons in compulsory subjects, for example, or insisting that they take physical exercise? The response comes under the 'leading a horse to water' principle. A teenager may choose not to engage wholeheartedly, but if he is not introduced and regularly encouraged, he is unlikely ever to participate.

The same holds true of compulsory assemblies and services of worship. Given half a chance the considerable majority of teenagers would opt out of chapel or assembly, not least because they tend to take place first thing in the morning. While Eton, like many boarding schools, happily provides services for Anglicans, Roman Catholics, Muslims, Jews, Hindus and Buddhists on a Sunday, the short weekday acts of worship are compulsory for all faiths and none. The prime significance of these gatherings is community – being together and belonging. The collective presence, taking time out of a busy day, listening to readings and music or simply allowing the mind to wander, creates a quality of experience different from the rest of the working day, and an opportunity for the spiritual dimension to flicker and be renewed. Formal religion is some way further down the list. I am regularly struck by the numbers of former pupils I meet, few of them religious in a conventional sense, who look back on their time in chapel with affection. They say it is a special place. It is special because what they have experienced there removed them from the mundane, briefly but regularly, and also took them out of their individual selves as part of a group, particularly in moments of silence.

Some teenagers are strongly drawn to spiritual truth revealed through an established religion. For believers, spirituality comes through the revealed word of God, which is the one and only 'given'. I have witnessed how this belief can give young people moral direction and a clear focus to their lives. At a time of uncertainty, the stronger the religious certainty, the greater the comfort. For some, this certainty will be a crutch to help them through a confusing time, for others their faith will be lifelong and a source of continuing wonder to them. Some among them will be fiercely protective of their faith: I have had occasional visits from pupils who tell me that chapel is not Christian enough and trenchant advocates of other faiths who wish to take themselves apart from the broader community. Young teenagers are at an impressionable age. Any pressure to create religious ghettos must be firmly resisted by schools. The spirit 'bloweth where it listeth' and is not the preserve of a self-appointed or chosen band.

A diet of one formal religion is often pretty off-putting to teenagers. It can feel didactic, limiting, even a dead hand. Their natural curiosity wants to test the claims of interpreters of the word. By contrast, it is notable how the young readily and enthusiastically engage with comparisons of religions. There is a deep desire to delve deeper and explore life beyond the physical. Interfaith work has been one of the great advances during my teaching career. Projects that bring together, say, a Hindu storyteller and a humanist, or a group of young people of different beliefs, or a Jew and a Muslim sharing a stage to discuss themes around justice, relationships and preparing for death, can have a lasting impact on teenagers. A well-run session taking a group of teenagers from different schools and different backgrounds away for a day can bring the most startling realization and awareness to each individual. It is one of the most powerful experiences of learning I have witnessed, more life-transforming than any one experience within the formal school curriculum.

Trawling the troubled waters around religion and spirituality has changed over the years. In this respect A. C. Benson speaks from an alien age. His concern about spirituality is about the extent to which formal church liturgy should be used in school. For the times he seems almost liberal in his belief that religion should attempt to come alongside the individual rather than the other way around, but the equation he draws between religion and the spirit is tight and absolute. A teacher should 'see that his own religion is simple and vital' and encourage pupils to be pilgrims and heroes, fighting the good fight.

More recent approaches see spiritual life as something distinct from religion. The argument for spiritual humanism resonates with many young people. Spiritual humanists would say that formal religion, science and material humanism have all missed the point. Religions, they say, started with highly charismatic individuals who had an experience beyond words. Subsequent attempts to express their experience in words reduces it; man ends up projecting his limited vocabulary and mindset on to a God figure. Man makes God in his image. Scientists, meanwhile, devise rules of thumb to help humans make some sense of reality. Like a series of Russian dolls they move from the material to the metaphysical, from matter to maths. Yet the failure of science, says the spiritual humanist, is that its powers of analysis are limited; there is a void where lies the unknown. Material humanists inhabit a similarly constrained position. Human beings are essentially pieces of carbon woven intricately by chance and time; humans are thus an extension of the material world.

For spiritual humanists, human beings cannot be described only as matter. Humans do not thrive simply by being compliant with a natural, physical order, but often in defiance of it, learning to stand up for themselves and, in so doing, moving civilization forward. Crucially what science cannot define is consciousness, man's state of understanding and awareness of the world around him. People do not just live with each other, they live *for* each other. That is a compelling message for the young, especially those doubtful that formal religion has much to offer them. Living for each other should underscore everything that schools seek to achieve.

Established religions are often poor at conveying their message, particularly to the young. Religion can seem formulaic, hidebound, aesthetically pleasing perhaps, but just a form of theatre, and a predictable one at that. High-flown rhetoric and reference to afterlife seem hard to take. Yet in the Christian tradition, for example, spiritual life is not held within boundaries dictated by ethereal religion, it is expressed in life. From roots in Judaism comes the idea that gatherings of people searching for justice and righteousness are a spiritual act. The Good Samaritan is the essence of spiritual life expressed in service to a stranger. This is an idea of spiritual life with which teenagers can readily identify. Service to the community is both social and spiritual.

Creeds constrain. The risk for formal religion is that it becomes a thing in itself, and is seen as such by the young, not a channel for the spirit. Creeds tend to be written after the charismatic individual has gone. It is a challenge for young people to consider whether Jesus would have wished for a formal creed at all.

For parents and teachers, the very heart of it is succinctly expressed in words from *Tales from the Hasidim* by Martin Buber. Rabbi Shelomo of Karlin poses the question, 'What is the worst thing the Evil urge can achieve?' To which he answers, 'To make men forget he is the child of a King.' This is an idea echoed in the Psalms: 'I will praise thee; for I am fearfully and wonderfully made' (Psalm 139:14, AV). A sense of wonder at oneself and one's life is the essential starting point for spiritual life.

Let there be wonder in our schools and let our children be wonderful.

9

Reading

'These days children do not have to be literate to achieve an apparent level of literacy.' So said an experienced primary school teacher. She drew my attention to the number of children who achieve respectable test scores but who are not able to cope at secondary level. Even then, she observed, only two-thirds of children are assessed as able to read at a fairly basic level of competence. 'We let down our children completely if they cannot read well.' She is right. Reading is at the very heart of our children's success at school.

A little background: the three R's

Received wisdom has it that the functional skills underpinning a good education are the three Rs – reading, (w)riting and (a)rithmetic. This formula gained popular currency in the early part of the nineteenth century but has echoes all the way back to St Augustine. It has been tinkered with over the years, most notably in the early Victorian period when a fourth R was identified: (w)righting (as in wheelwrighting), a reference to skilled work with the hands which we might now refer to as the vocational route. This vocational R fell out of fashion, possibly under the influence of high-minded public schools with their stress on the Classics. In any event, by the end of the century the distinction between the academic and vocational was sharply drawn and, to our discredit, has remained with us ever since.

Other intruders have sought to break into the harmony of the three Rs. For some in America, for example, religion is seen as a functional skill. Yet the historic trio still presents itself as the core of an effective education, giving pride of place to young people's ability to understand ideas through words and number. Contemporary candidates for inclusion might be relearning or resilience; but even so, it is hard to shake off the belief that facility in word and number is the cornerstone for everything else.

I am often assailed by critics (mostly of an older generation) who are convinced that standards are not what they were, that teenagers can no longer do basic maths or write intelligibly – and that they do not read. From my perspective the situation is rather different. The problem lies in the phrase 'no longer'. It has always been the case that too many of our young population have found difficulty developing their functional skills. There was no golden age. At times in the past a relatively small group of school pupils was able to deal elegantly with word and number – and that is true today.

Progress has been patchy, but there are some good signs. By international comparison, the mathematical capacity of British teenagers seems to lag behind many others in the developed world, and there are significant problems with the supply of good maths teachers, yet the teaching of maths has been increasingly effective; that maths is now a popular subject choice at A Level in many schools would have been unthinkable when I began my teaching career. Less exam content has made maths more accessible to more students and I have seen more inventive teaching focused on the individual's understanding of number than I ever recall from my own schooldays. This is not a case of 'dumbing down', but of being more inventive.

As an English teacher, however, reading and writing concern me. Handwriting as a popular habit is in terminal decline. At exam time it is easy to see the problem: one script I have seen returned after A Level showed a candidate under pressure resorting in desperation to inscribing a series of straight lines of differing lengths punctuated with the odd dot, like a jumbled form of Morse code. It takes deeply ingrained and well-rehearsed skills in handwriting to be able to shape words consistently and clearly under timed conditions. At present we face a strange mismatch: teenagers for whom the keyboard is natural have to write by hand in a public examination. Perhaps the Morse code exam answer marks the boundary between the old and new.

Most teenagers' ability to write swiftly and competently at a computer screen is truly remarkable to someone of my age. I am not convinced that there has been any diminution in teenagers' ability to deal with the mechanics of writing, but it is increasingly done by using a different medium. When it comes to exams, either schools will need to impose a moratorium on writing by computer some weeks before the exam season so that pupils may have practice in their handwriting skills, or, more likely, exams will be taken online, though the latter poses daunting logistical and technical challenges.

I would like to think that there will always be a place for the handwritten word. The individuality of character expressed through the hand cannot properly be matched by machine, especially when it comes to expressing gratitude. A quick 'thank you' by email seems too casual and impersonal. This may, however, be the last stand of hand-crafted writing. An ability for people to touch-type will come to be seen as a great deal more important than shaping curves and lines. Elegant handwriting will, however, by virtue of its rarity become the more prized: it could become a specialized career like the medieval scribe's. As so often, regression is part of progression. We will lose something of the aesthetic value of handwriting, but the important thing is that school-aged children learn to write readily with clarity and precision. The medium must fit the needs of the time.

This is also true of grammar. It is a standard gibe in a teachers' common room that English teachers do not have a grasp of English grammar: linguists or, especially, classicists are the people to ask if you have a query about sub-clauses or the subjunctive. Particularly since the 1960s English teachers have been more focused on a child's ability to communicate thoughts and emotions through writing, than on grammatical details which some see as a curb on creativity. This makes sense – up to a point. At its worst, however, English teaching has declined into a self-indulgent cod-psychology where being in touch with feelings is the only 'truth' and where ideas about form and structure have no place.

Rules of grammar exist for a purpose. There is a grammar in all intellectual disciplines: a grammar of maths, chemistry and history as much as English. Grammar is the backbone of thought. Yet while the grammar in maths is taught clearly and openly, most English teachers will back away from such a direct approach, and they are right to do so. This apparently strange anomaly is resolved when the skill of writing is learnt through reading. The best English teachers will walk alongside a pupil on their route through an imagined landscape, sharing delight and even wonder at what they have seen, and only then showing how a literary effect is created by the dextrous use of rhythm or the deliberate subverting of grammatical rules or clever play with tropes. It is at this stage that students often take pleasure in how it all works, like seeing the intricate mechanism of a clock, better still taking it to pieces and putting it back again. Learning slabs of grammar has something of the train-spotter about it, detail for detail's sake.

What becomes clear is just how important is the ability for a child to read comfortably, intelligently and for a sustained period of time. It is the bedrock of education. OECD research shows that reading for pleasure is a more important influence than socio-economic background (2002) and that children who read for pleasure have a one and a half year advantage on their peers (2011).

I have no doubt that the greatest gift a parent can give to their child's schooling and future prospects is the ability to read well before starting formal school. It is a parental gift because the best route to a lifelong intimacy with reading is regular reading sessions involving both parent and small child. A child imbibes the significance and fun of reading most naturally from parents. In many cases this will mean repeating the same story over and over again as the child links the shapes in front of her to the sound she hears. It can seem a frustrating, even time-wasting activity for busy parents, but it is crucial. The time spent sitting down quietly and sharing a story is time very well invested. A child starting school unable to read will be playing catch-up. There is no substitute for the many hours a young child spends experimenting with language and the written word.

Primary

In the primary school world, 'literacy' has been the subject of various schemes and strategies in recent years. As with most aspects of learning, attempts to bolt on a module or carve out a slice of time to accelerate progress have met with, at best, partial success because effective learning is interwoven with a school's whole culture. Primary teachers tend to be rather dismissive of the 'literacy hour', for example, understanding that a child's ability to read and write well has to be encouraged throughout the curriculum.

Experienced primary school teachers stress five key points about children and reading:

1. Children benefit from having books read aloud to them. Children need to have many stories read to them before they cut loose and read for themselves, and there is not enough reading aloud to children in schools. Some children will not sit down and read a book until they are much older.

2. Children should be allowed to choose their own books as far as possible. As a young teacher I believed that children should be reared on a rich diet of good reading, but I realize that any reading has nutrition. It is inculcating a habit that matters. Judgement and taste will develop from the earliest years, but enjoyment must come first. That said,

young children can understand that persevering
with a text they do not particularly like has value as
reading practice, providing the adult is honest about
it and accepts their feelings.

3. Children should always be encouraged to have
   a go and not worry about misreading and
   mispronunciation. They should be drawn into
   conversations about what they have read, although
   this takes skill, patience and the capacity to
   decode, because young children are keen to please
   and give the answer they think the adult wants.
   Learning to consider and state a personal view
   takes confidence.

4. Parents need to understand that being literate is
   not the same thing as being literary. Many adults
   harbour respect for particular genres they feel are
   appropriate or which they judge will set a child's
   imagination alight. Story reading is powerful for
   many children, but others are relieved to be told
   that it is quite all right to read non-fiction.

5. Schools need to be robust in ensuring that children
   have to read instructions for themselves, whether
   information sheets or web pages, about each and
   every subject in school. Reading must permeate every
   part of a child's life. An adult reading out maths
   instructions, for example, is too easy a short cut. In
   this regard, labelling a set text as a 'reading book' can

be counter-productive as it allows a child to perceive the business of reading as an isolated subject.

The disparity in standards of literacy among pupils entering secondary school at age 11 is staggering and the burden placed on secondary school teachers to accommodate a wide range of ability on this most fundamental of skills can be overwhelming. The surest way to raise standards nationally is to create a firm base of competency in reading from the earliest years. This requires a school culture in which the ability to read eagerly and well is the prime goal, more significant even than numeracy targets or facility in writing. With confidence in reading the written word, the world becomes a map of possibilities and adventure. Without it, the journey is down a long street with doors closed on either side.

Teenagers and reading

How can we engage teenagers in reading? What should we expect of them? What should they read?

When talking to teachers who have been successful in engaging reluctant teenagers to read, it is striking how many of the themes and remedies identified by primary school teachers hold true.

Like young children, teenagers need to be encouraged to read anything and everything. Even the 'cornflakes' test can be revealing – does your bleary-eyed child read the text on the side of the cereal packet at breakfast? The reading habit is a muscle that needs to be exercised daily.

Generalized encouragement can, however, simply prove an irritation to a teenager who lacks motivation or feels threatened by an activity that is onerous. There is no escaping the fact that it is essential to raise levels of competency before tackling motivation. It is difficult for anyone to enjoy an activity when they do not feel confident about their ability. Anxious parents can sometimes resort to full-frontal nagging, an approach guaranteed to harden a teenager's resolve not to participate.

The problems tend to be more marked with teenage boys. There is some evidence that girls respond to the written word more readily, a consequence of both hardwiring and culture. Even today, reading is deemed by some (not least boys) to be a more suitable occupation for a girl. Whatever the reason, many teenage boys just do not want to waste time reading. Quite often, boys who find reading a chore have been asked to read books beyond their capability, and if reading holds little inherent interest for them, the whole exercise will have seemed pointless. They will need to be redirected to material that has some meaning for them. Talking with the boy is the necessary starting point, finding out how much he reads, what sort of material he enjoys and what topics interest him. Electronic devices and browsing the internet can help. A relaxed approach starting from individual interest can be a welcome relief for boys who may have been bombarded with books that are just too hard.

Many boys have picked up the message that fiction is the only 'proper' type of reading. Over the years I have seen many boys led to lasting enjoyment of fiction by alternative routes, through magazines, websites, eBooks, newspapers, poetry, manuals, short stories, graphic novels, comics and even puzzle books. Being told that these alternative texts are important reading material can be both a revelation and an encouragement. Tackling more challenging and more rewarding literature can come later.

I enjoy talking with teachers who are really good at what they do. Here are five points from teachers gifted in raising the reading levels and the expectations of teenage boys. These are professional 'notes to self', but they offer a steer to anxious parents, too.

1. Value reading aloud. Reading aloud can be seen to be a primary school activity, but it is worthwhile throughout a teenager's school career. Listening attentively is a skill which may well need development.

2. Show that choice matters; all reading is good. It is best to respect boys' preferences and start from their personal interests.

3. Think about how best to introduce a specific author or series of books. I have seen the effect that an adult or friend can have on boys by reading a section of text aloud to them. They become interested enough to read on, either by

themselves or sharing the reading with others. Part of the aim when sharing reading with boys is to increase their reading stamina. Books are written to be read as a whole and it is important where possible to enable boys to read books as complete texts. This can be achieved through paired or shared reading, or by using short stories, many of which are short enough to be read in one sitting, which is a significant boon to a reader with a memory weakness.

4. Encourage poetry and plays as a way in. Poetry and rhyme work well with many young people, be it the work of an established poet or raps and song lyrics. Karaoke can provide an unobtrusive reading opportunity. Seeing a play before reading it aids recall and understanding. Subsequently reading the play aloud in groups gives a boost to confidence and fluency.

5. Make it fun. A wealth of reading material helps: novels, biographies, magazines, comics, non-fiction, short stories. There will be a magazine or journal to touch on any interest a boy is likely to have and the material does not have to be read sequentially, but can be dipped into and browsed. The aim is to motivate. Alternative forms of reading can break a prejudice against the book: iPods, kindles, downloads, e-readers and the like. Boys can be reassured that it is acceptable to pick up a book and not read beyond the first few pages if it holds no

intrinsic appeal. Negative perceptions are reinforced
if a boy has to plough on with something he does
not enjoy and feels under pressure to finish.

In sum, with reluctant teenage readers the key is to
develop a habit of reading by whatever means and
through whichever medium or material. Everything else –
discernment, awareness of genres, perseverance with
challenging texts or literary taste, stems from that.

If all goes well, teenagers should be able to hear the
voice of the writing as they read. Some teenagers put up a
roadblock when they reach a point of mechanical literacy.
They have enough, as they see it, to get by and need
persuasion to go further. Going further should be the aim
of all schools. Engendering a habit of reading widely and
regularly for study and for pleasure should be axiomatic as
part of a broad-based education. As the habit develops, so
too should the ability to make value judgements about the
quality of the writing. The capacity to read independently
for meaning rather than needing to be directed, to
connect with the thoughts of fictional characters, to read
a world inside one's head, to analyse arguments and weigh
up situations, are all prerequisites of a fulfilled adult life.
We speak of reading books, but we also speak of reading
situations and people. Adults become useful citizens when
they know how to make their way in society and have the
developed skill of empathy to interpret the people and
events around them.

One of the most effective ways to encourage teenagers to read deeply is through collaboration. For many boys, in particular, being expected to sit quietly alone and wade through a lengthy text is a request too far. Old-fashioned though it sounds, a teenage version of the book club can work well. Giving boys a choice, for example, of two novels of no more than three hundred pages in length which will lead to small-group discussion brings some shape and intent to the business of reading. Best of all are the conversations between adult and teenager, especially in an informal moment, which pick up shared points of interest or enquiry.

An alternative is for a group of teenagers to choose a novel, say one for each half-term, which leads to a gathering to which an interested adult is invited. The combination of structure and the fresh impetus of an adult new to them can lead to a lively and enjoyable discussion. These approaches are easier to arrange in a school but I have seen similar ideas play well with groups of parents. The key, they tell me, is not having parent and child in the same group.

The range of texts from which to choose is wide. Some suggestions of texts that work well include *The Curious Incident of the Dog in the Night-Time*, *The Absolutist*, *The Rosie Project* and *Butcher's Crossing*. These novels work well on different levels and are popular throughout the teenage years.

Many parents are convinced that the ability of teenagers to read for deeper meaning is being hindered by electronic communication and the internet. It is a well-placed worry. It is not that the demise of the book would mean the end of literature, because other media will develop as vehicles for the imagination and may, indeed, stimulate new styles and forms of writing. The issue is *how* we read and expect teenagers to read.

Some fifty years ago, the advent of television provoked a chorus of dismay in the widespread belief that reading would suffer. This has not proven to be the case at all. In fact in a way once not thought possible, sales of literary texts that have been televised have risen significantly. Far from being in mutual antipathy, visual image and written word have complemented each other.

The e-age, however, changes that relationship in one crucial respect. A quick fix of sound bites, snippets and tweets invites a short attention span, and that can become an attraction in itself. If a website is not immediately accessible it is, by instant definition, a bad page. A regular diet of quick fixes erodes the capacity and the desire to read for a sustained period of time and, by extension, the capacity for sustained argument and study.

What is not self-evident, however, is that one approach necessarily snuffs out the other. In the future, it is possible that young people will see their electronic device as the only source of reference. Even if that is the case, it is also possible that teenagers will be able to deal happily with the same device in different ways. Teenagers readily learn to use more than one register of speech and writing. Most teenagers, indeed, jealously guard the parameters of teenage life, which is why they dislike having their parents sharing social media. They develop their own shorthand and often a patois to heighten their sense of their identity as a group separate from the adult world. There is nothing new in this; most parents will recall the slang and private references of their own teenage years. Teenagers will seek out new and exciting ways to be private, communicating through the latest app that flares into life and then dies only to be replaced by the next fad.

Yet it is perfectly possible for them to associate the different registers they use in school, at home, and in the adult world with alternative uses of their e-device. Reading a long novel on the screen requires a different mindset, one that is developed through habit. All reading requires training and practice. Reading online is a skill in itself which should be taught and encouraged in schools, alongside traditional printed text.

Reading targets for teenagers

Young people will learn at their own pace and in their own time and teachers and parents need to be wary about how misleading templates can be. I have seen too many cases of young people deemed 'behind' in some area of their intellectual development, who then go on to blossom in later years, for me to worry too much that a child has failed to meet an arbitrary target. Nonetheless, it can be helpful to have markers along the way.

What follows are guidelines that indicate what intelligent young people should be capable of achieving through the teenage years.

At 13, above all, boys and girls should be able to move beyond basic functional literacy and read for meaning and pleasure, both in school and on their own. They should be able actively to develop their vocabulary for reading and writing, seeking out new words and playing with language. They should be able to read aloud fluently and with expression as well as following a text aurally that someone else is reading out (with and without seeing it). In short, it is at the outset of the teenage years that the habit of reading should be deeply rooted.

Among other things, a boy or girl of this age should be able to identify different genres of writing, to be able to sift relevant facts and arguments from the irrelevant, and to identify main points and generalizations. They should also be comfortable using a library catalogue and finding information online; and they need to understand the nature of plagiarism.

At 16, boys and girls should be able to read with concentration and stamina. They should be able to summarize accurately what they have read and predict the outcome of a line of thought and draw conclusions from it. The prerequisites for a lifetime of sustained, effective reading should now be in place. Their critical skills should be developed to the point that they can identify propositions and arguments and spot abuses of argument, such as fallacies. This critical facility should also be applied to the internet, so that they can evaluate and use the information they come across; they also need to understand that an ethical code applies when using the internet just as much as with printed texts.

At 18, they should have developed their ability to study to an advanced level based on the firm foundation of reading skills. They should be able, for example, to use primary and secondary sources, cross-refer on the internet, write a bibliography correctly, and use index pages and search facilities efficiently.

Books to read

Any good school will provide useful lists of books to read. Tastes vary and judgements differ and it is a given that no choice will command universal support, but I find it helpful to ask experienced teachers which books they think have particular impact on their pupils.

What follows is a list of books, listed by subject discipline, that are key texts to challenge and inspire inquisitive, intelligent 16-year-olds. Indeed, I am tempted to say that the well-educated, ambitious teenage polymath should read them all.

Books every bright 16-year-old should read

Literature

Gulliver's Travels, Jonathan Swift
David Copperfield, Charles Dickens
Heart of Darkness, Joseph Conrad
The Age of Innocence, Edith Wharton
Atonement, Ian McEwan
Never Let Me Go, Kazuo Ishiguro
The Bonfire of the Vanities, Tom Wolfe

Literature in translation

French:
L'élégance du hérisson, Muriel Barbery (The Elegance of the Hedgehog)

Spanish:
La sombra del viento, Carlos Ruiz Zafón (The Shadow of the Wind)

German:
Tschick, Wolfgang Herrndorf (Why We Took the Car)

Russian:
The Master and Margarita, Mikhail Bulgakov

Italian:
Il sentiero dei nidi di ragno, Italo Calvino (The Path to the Nest of Spiders)

Portuguese:
O Crime do Padre Amaro, José Maria de Eça de Queirós
(The Sin/Crime of Father Amaro)

Japanese:
Hard-boiled Wonderland and the End of the World, Haruki
Murakami

Chinese:
Wolf Totem, Jiang Rong

Arabic:
Beirut 39, Samuel Shimon and Hanan Al-Shaykh (a
collection of short stories)

Science

Bad Science, Ben Goldacre
Genome, Matt Ridley
Six Easy Pieces, Richard Feynman

Philosophy

Sophie's World, Jostein Gaarder

Ethics

Rethinking Life and Death, Peter Singer

Theology

The Case for Religion, Keith Ward
The Sea of Faith, Don Cupitt

History of Art

Michelangelo and the Pope's Ceiling, Ross King
The Story of Art, Ernst Gombrich

Art

Blimey! – From Bohemia to BritPop, Matthew Collings
The Horse's Mouth, Joyce Carey

History

The First Crusade: The Call From The East, Peter Frankopan
The Realities Behind Diplomacy, Paul Kennedy

Economics

Almost Everyone's Guide to Economics, J. K. Galbraith
The Affluent Society, Galbraith

Politics

In Defence of Politics, Bernard Crick

Geography

The Power of Place: Geography, Destiny and Globalisation's Rough Landscape, Harm de Blij
On the Map: A Mind-expanding Exploration of the Way the World Looks, Simon Garfield

Classics

The Iliad, Homer, trans. Martin Hammond
Confronting the Classics: Traditions, Adventures and Innovations, Mary Beard

Mathematics

To Infinity and Beyond: A Cultural History of the Infinite, Eli Maor
Algorithmics: The Spirit of Computing, David Harel and Yishai Feldman

Music

Music: A Very Short Introduction, Nicholas Cook

Design

The Language of Things, Deyan Sudjic

Advice to parents

As a parent I would be keen to see the reading policy of my child's school, not least to establish if there is one, and I would ask how it is monitored. Each head of an academic department should be able to demonstrate how the habit of deep reading is inculcated in their work and how they measure pupils' success. Each department should be able to offer specific advice on wider reading to extend a pupil's vocabulary and understanding of the subject, and show how they actively use libraries and the internet to promote reading.

More generally, I would ask whether pupils are expected to keep an online reading journal which records their own choice of reading throughout their school careers or whether other logs, such as 'commonplace' books, are encouraged. I would also ask whether school reports refer to their reading.

The point is that reading needs to be nurtured and placed centre stage throughout a school career. All too often, this most essential of skills and habits is assumed to be developing quietly and untended. This can sometimes be the case; rather more frequently it is not.

In his essay 'Of Studies' published in 1625, Francis Bacon wrote that discussion sharpens the wits and writing hones precision, but it is 'Reading maketh a full man'. Reading still really matters.

10

Turning it Around

Slough is a fascinating place. It is true that it is an unlovely town associated most readily with the grim roundabout in the opening credits of 'The Office' or Betjeman's invocation, 'Come friendly bombs and fall on Slough/ It isn't fit for humans now'. When my wife first bought a train ticket from Paddington to Slough, she was told by the attendant, 'We should pay you to go there, love.' Yet it is a kaleidoscope of cultures and world views, just a short walk from the playing fields of Eton.

Though located in East Berkshire, Slough has greater affinity with the East End of London. Indeed, Slough and Newham are statistical neighbours. Among the welter of facts and figures about Slough the diversity shows through. According to the 2011 census Slough has the highest concentration of Sikhs in the country, the second-highest proportion of Pakistanis, and just one-third of the population are 'white British'. Perhaps the real measure of diversity is the fact that just over half (56 per cent) of the people in Slough have all household members of the same ethnic group – and average household size is the second-highest in the country. Just 61 per cent of residents were born in the UK (by comparison with 87 per cent nationwide) and about the same number (60.5 per cent) evince no sense of English identity. From the point of view of schooling, a low proportion of households (67 per cent) have English as the main language for all members. This could well be the description of an inner London borough. There are two significant differences, however: Slough retains selection at 11+ so the non-grammar school comprehensives face similar challenges to the old secondary modern schools; and Slough attracts none of the additional funding available to London boroughs. The funding differential is significant: Hounslow borders Slough and is a similar-sized education authority, yet receives £178 million in comparison to Slough's £113 million. Inner city Newham receives over £300 million. Taking on a failing school in Slough is a daunting prospect.

This is what Paul McAteer did in 2004. Langleywood School, as it was then called, is situated to the east of Slough, serving a mix of young people from a variety of ethnic backgrounds with about half of them 'white British'. Before 2004, the culture of the school was negative and forbidding. Locally, the school had become a byword for complacency and despair and had fallen into special measures for the second time. As tends to happen, when standards and ethos unravel, the school can all too quickly fall into the grip of spiralling decline. Most of the teachers were on short-term contracts. Parents who were able to do so moved their children.

The atmosphere was tense. Paul's first sports day was marked by aggressive truancy – boys and girls who absented themselves chose to return to throw bricks at the competitors. One girl, enjoying a cigarette with friends, identified the new head and greeted him with the observation, 'You won't effing last.'

What Paul discovered was not unique. It does not take much for a community to regress into dysfunction: there is a touch of *Lord of the Flies* in all of us. When I am asked for Eton's secret, my answer is simple: it works because, in very large measure, the teenagers I work with want to make it work. Without their broad support, any head is in serious trouble.

At Langleywood, many teenagers clearly had no interest in making it work. As has been reported increasingly in the past 20 years, some of the most entrenched disaffection and antagonism comes from the white British, particularly from what some describe as the 'non-working' or 'dependency' class. Where there is no respect for the very idea of education, it is hard to chart a path forward. In one primary school in Slough, for example, where parents were inclined to be dressed in pyjamas when they dropped off their children, the swifter to return to bed, there was a fundamental conflict of social attitude to negotiate. The school made great efforts to persuade bellicose youngsters to talk through their issues with others, only to discover that the child prepared to reason had been physically beaten at home for failing to stand up for himself. These were the kind of households where parents forbade pens and pencils at home, somewhat constraining the notion of homework, because they assumed that the child would scribble on the walls.

The impasse is nothing new. Low standards and low aspirations breed complacency and inertia. Low self-esteem breeds despair and aggression. As an aspirant candidate for teacher training in the 1970s, I was sent for two weeks of lesson observation in what was, in effect, a secondary modern. The first teacher I met welcomed me with the words 'This is a crap school, mine is a crap class, and I am a crap teacher.' He was right, at least on the last point.

Coming in to the maelstrom of a failing school is tough. For a start, it can feel physically intimidating. Public perception and the law, rightly, are weighted in favour of the young, but many adults can be undermined and left vulnerable in a school environment in which there do not appear to be parameters of behaviour. Paul McAteer is a plain-speaking man. He has no doubt about the crucial, non-negotiable first step in turning around a failing school: an intense focus on behaviour.

Paul took up his three-year contract with the brief of bringing the school to a point of stability to enable it to be transformed into an academy: if he failed, the school could be closed. As he began, a national newspaper greeted him with the headline, 'Is Langleywood the worst school in

Britain?' In retrospect the publicity proved a bonus. Paul needed to build an effective and reliable team quickly. In addition to having a high proportion of teachers on temporary contracts, the school had been spending some £200,000 a year just on supply teachers to fill the gaps, over 5 per cent of the overall budget. Sounding out his contacts through London Challenge and elsewhere was, Paul says, like recruiting the Magnificent Seven. The challenge proved a spur and he was able to recruit 20 new teachers on full contracts.

And so began the relentless focus on discipline, with the head personally taking the lead. By bearing down on details one at a time (the wearing of a necktie, the prohibition of swearing, a ban on hoodies ...), by stating expectations clearly to parents through newsletters, by following through with exclusions whatever the parental bullying, Paul and his team achieved the consistency which is the foundation stone of an effective school. Parents and pupils were made to realize that there were fixed standards and no backing down. Following an exclusion, pupils were only allowed to return to the school if parents took time off work and came for an interview with the head. It was the simple law of cause and effect made real.

Paul would be the first to acknowledge that his approach is far from new or ground-breaking, but it was ground-breaking in that school at that time. To hear Paul speak of his insistence on tidy hair (not less than a No. 2 cut, no patterns etc.) is an echo of the West London

comprehensive head who told me his school survived the
excesses of student radicalism in 1968 by dint of the head
drawing the battleground over hair length. Rebellions were
fierce but largely centred on the relatively trivial business
of hairstyles.

In his third year at Langleywood, shortly before it was
to be transformed into the multi-million-pound Norman
Foster-designed Langley Academy, Paul invited me to
present the prizes. Prize Days are often a good test of a
school culture – not the winning and receiving (though
pupils' choice of prize can be illuminating) but the
atmosphere of the event. On the evidence of that evening,
Langleywood had come a long way. Boys and girls seemed
to want to be there (and, indeed, were actually present);
there was generous applause for the achievements of
others and a sense of purpose, of looking to the future
with enthusiasm. An attempt at prize-giving in the first
year had not been a success, marked by swagger, sneering
thuggishness and an absence of parents. On this finale
for Langleywood the parent body, at least in part, was
engaged.

At times it feels as though my life has been measured
out by school prize-givings. They tend to fade into a
jumbled memory as one seamless long event. They follow
a ritual pattern, a youthful dance to the rhythm of parental
applause. Some of these events stand out; the little prep
school, for example, where it was clear early on that the
genial elderly teacher handing me the prizes to pass on

to the children had muddled them up – it took some persuading to encourage the winner of the senior chess competition to accept a plastic red double-decker bus. Most striking, though, was the comprehensive in inner-city Birmingham where the first people to come forward to accept their certificates were some mothers who had been taking a course back in school. It seems a simple thing, but it spoke volumes. This school community had taken seriously its commitment to engage parents with the life of the school and to use them as a statement of intent. The applause from the children as parents came up to receive their prizes was deafening. It felt like a school with momentum and drive.

A few streets away from the railway station in Slough is St Joseph's Catholic High School. This was a school that ticked over in a modest way for years, enough to escape the attentions of critical inspectors or extra government funding. Visiting was like stepping back to the school of my teaching-practice days, shabby and under-resourced, but coping. Surprisingly, it had achieved 'Good' status in an Ofsted inspection, though it did not feel 'good'. It was an example of the parts being valued as more than the sum, a school that could be ticked off against certain headings but where the ethos was flat and loose. A glance at a whole-school photograph of that period is revealing: the staff look ahead at the camera, behind them boys and girls adopt a variety of postures while wearing their school uniform in inventive ways.

A new head tried to introduce changes but the old guard were not with him. Slipping to 'Satisfactory' on inspection, followed by financial crisis, was enough for the head to lose his job and for the old guard to jettison his changes. Life would return to normal. On one level things seemed to be going well; the school was placed in the top 100 improving schools in the country based on raw attainment statistics. Not for the first time, the statistics were misleading. The next Ofsted inspection picked this up and the school's status slipped again to 'Requires Improvement'. As can happen, a year or two of misfortune with changes to the school leadership and mismanaged finances had brought the school pretty much to its knees.

Ciran Stapleton, the third head in as many years, had just completed his first year when we spoke about turning a school around. The most striking feature of the school, he felt, was the culture among the teaching staff. What he saw were a crucial trio of professional qualities all lacking: accountability, responsibility and ownership. There was a general sense that being nice to the children was sufficient, expectations of achievement were low, there was little homework set or marked, and discipline was poor. Yet many of the staff, particularly the senior staff, clung on to memories of the previous 'good' inspection result and saw no need to change.

Inspection is important, but it can be a two-edged weapon. By focusing on a limited range of measurable outcomes it is quite possible to miss the bigger picture. To be told by a visiting inspector that she was not interested in the ethos of the school but only the statistics was, for Ciran, a depressing moment. Without a strong and purposeful ethos, a school culture is planted in thin soil.

Although the inspection process is designed to force schools to lift their eyes to the horizon and see themselves clearly, staff and governors at St Joseph's believed their own myth. To the outside eye this was a school in trouble, one in which the staff seemed to believe the school was shaped around their needs, not the needs of the children. To the long-serving insider the rhythm of the school was much as it had always been: recent local difficulties would be resolved, an objectionable, demanding new head would be seen off and life would continue as before.

Ciran found a potent cocktail of self-delusion and demoralization. The school he inherited had spent £164,000 on cover expenses for staff who had been absent for 484 days in the previous school year. There were more requests for absence in his first three weeks in charge than there had been in his previous seven years in senior management.

The starting point was to create a senior leadership team committed to change. This he did by moving some teachers into roles for which they were better suited and by bringing in new blood. Rather as with Paul McAteer's recruitment of the 'Magnificent Seven', the parlous state of the school was an attraction to young, ambitious and enthusiastic leaders. The difference between my visits to the school was striking. While the problems remain the same, the energy of the new leadership team touches every aspect of school life, the school is calm and ordered and there is a sense of momentum and direction.

How has this turnaround been achieved? There is the same unrelenting insistence on small matters of discipline that underpinned the transformation at Langleywood. From my own experience, I would not underestimate the vigour and dedication required to pin down these details day after day as a necessary war of attrition is waged. In the classroom, there is also a vigorous campaign. In the absence of a shared, positive culture to achieving high standards, adopting a subtle coaching style does not work. The approach is unashamedly institutional, even if 'it goes against the grain'. Targets are clearly stated, to the extent that they appear on large notices in sight of everyone in the classroom. These, Ciran notes, are not targets for the sake of having targets, but a means to an end, to inculcate accountability in each class. The real war in Ciran's eyes is against an undemanding and patronizing view of the relationship between teacher and pupil, where reputations are low, redolent of the 1980s.

A telling example of this attitude was the teacher, noted for lack of ambition at St Joseph's, who took a job at an expensive independent school, telling the head that people paying expensive fees had a right to expect high standards. The implication was clear: so too is Ciran's anger as he recounts the story. He wants a school driven by passion and integrity.

Integrity lies at the heart of an effective senior leadership team and thus of the school. When Ciran took up his post he was greeted by little open hostility but by the avoidance tactics of senior colleagues who whispered in corners and appeared to hope that he would go away. He felt it was crucial to have senior leaders who would assume nothing ('assumption is the mother of all cock-ups'), people who would join him in walking the corridors, using formal address to teachers in front of pupils, being direct and honest and holding themselves and others to account. As he recruited and shaped his new team he looked for people who had worked in successful schools, shared his values and ambition, and who, in his words, 'knew what a good school really looks like'.

The leadership of any school is a constant work in progress and the prospect of everything unravelling in spectacular fashion is the ever-present fear that keeps a head focused. The change of tone and organization at St Joseph's gives good cause for hope that the young people for whom the school exists will be properly served.

Paul McAteer clearly feels some attraction to Slough. From Langleywood he went on to Slough and Eton School, now renamed Slough and Eton Church of England Business and Enterprise College. Slough and Eton is the school in closest proximity to Eton, built on land once owned by Eton College and now separated by the M4. It is just a mile away but feels much further. It is one of those apparent anomalies, a Church of England school without Anglicans; with most of the pupil body being Muslim. Situated in Chalvey, 97 per cent of pupils are from ethnic minorities: its 3 per cent white pupils are East European.

On an early visit to Slough and Eton I had found the front door barred, not by a hostile group intent on preventing a public school head from entering, but by an armed man holding the receptionist at knife-point and effectively shutting down the school. It was a dramatic event but not wholly unexpected. Over the years there were improvements and I was able to test the water at their first prize-giving: there was just one book in English, a biography of David Beckham, and half the students called were absent, but it was a step forward. When Paul took over as head the school had reached 'Good' in its most recent inspection. This, in Paul's view, was to make the business of school improvement that much the harder.

Rather as Ciran had found, there was a need to tackle the school's own myth. As I have seen so often, the complacency that has blighted too many of our schools is born of the comforting belief that 'we do pretty well, considering...' The considerations are variously either poor facilities, feeble parenting, difficult children, incompetent leadership, or all of the above. Paul will have none of it. To walk around his school with him is to see how significant the physical presence of a head can be. Everyone knows who he is and they know and respect him, too. He has introduced little rituals such as five words for the week: challenging new words which every pupil must know and understand and which spark lively conversation with him in the lunch queue.

However, Paul had another difficult issue with which to deal, an entrenched and aggressive governing body. Being a school head is rather like playing three-dimensional chess. There are multiple constituencies of parents, teachers and pupils with which to deal, each with its own agenda which can shift and turn with the wind. This is a complicated landscape in which to plot a path but it is one made altogether tougher when the governing body is at odds with the head, or with itself. One head of an independent school who was facing criticism and difficulties told me that it had never occurred to him that a head needed to cultivate his own governing body. He had assumed they would be trenchant in support of the direction set by the head.

With changes in legislation devolving more legal responsibility to governors, it is perhaps understandable that some schools have found it hard to recruit governors who have both the desire and the necessary skills. It would seem money well spent for the state to provide funding for a paid clerk for every state school governing body in the land. A paid official would be able to chart difficult terrain and give reassurance to amateurs. A dispassionate official would also help avert some destructive, and costly situations. Part of the problem is that most of those who would entertain the idea of shouldering a governor's responsibility are likely to have some specific or emotional connection to the school. That is why it is common to find governing bodies populated by former or current parents and past pupils. The loyalty and passion they bring can prove an inspiration to the head, but their enthusiasm can tilt into dangerous territory, particularly when there is an issue at stake that strikes close to home. Governors who allow partiality, whose intent is to secure the best deal for their own children, for example, can not only contaminate the collegial atmosphere of a governing body, but also prove a brake on progress.

So it was at Slough and Eton. The formal process of investigating and, as it turned out, removing the governing body was time-consuming and painful, but wholly necessary. A good set of governors can help drive a school to greater heights and keep it there; as a body, they should be the critical friend of the head, holding himself and themselves accountable for the welfare and progress of the children entrusted to them. Far too often, governing bodies are battlegrounds in which cliques of self-interest vie with each other. Governance, in both state and independent schools, is a source of strength but has the potential to be a catastrophic liability.

I have always found it a pleasure to talk with people in my trade, wherever their school is located and whichever form it may take. As a new, young head of an independent school towards the end of the Thatcher era, I received a letter from the nearby comprehensive school making it clear that, as far as they were concerned, I was persona non grata and would not be welcomed on their site. Thanks in large measure to the greater autonomy afforded to heads in the state sector, many of these barriers have come down. There is an openness of conversation between fellow heads that must be beneficial to all of us, and to our pupils.

I greatly admire the work of Paul and Ciran and others like them. I learn from them, too. On the face of it our jobs could not be more different – they have turned around underperforming or failing state day schools. I took on a well-established, high-achieving, independent boarding school. Yet it is often by placing oneself in alien circumstances that one can learn most. In the same way that I have learnt more from an excellent PE lesson about the logistics of classroom management than I have ever gleaned from fellow English teachers, so I have held up my practice to the light when I see people like Paul or Ciran in action.

I have come properly to appreciate, for example, that refocusing sharply on what matters most is the most effective way to manage the competing demands of school life. When a school is in serious trouble, it is relatively clear what needs to happen. It is seeing it through to the end that takes real skill and dedication. When a school appears to be going well, however, it is easy to be seduced by the self-image that all established communities tend to project and often believe. A culture of constructive self-criticism is of great value to schools. The description 'great school' is sometimes used of the more famous public schools, in part a nod to history but also a reflection of their own sense of self and their ambition. However, paradox though it may seem, a 'great school' may not be a very good school at all. Well-known public schools can be just as guilty of complacency, self-delusion and the tacit assumption that the school exists primarily for the comfort of the teaching staff as any other school. 'Never believe your own myth' is an axiom of the utmost relevance to public and state school heads alike.

Two other qualities I particularly admire in Paul and Ciran are their eye for detail and sheer stamina. A high-performing school can be sustained by institutional momentum for a while. Heads in the business of turning around a school have no such luxury. They must necessarily concentrate on getting the basics right day by day – and that requires a deep well of energy from which to draw.

Coming to run a successful school brings a different set of challenges, not least understanding the multiple layers of expectation and perception held by different parts of the school community. Yet the clarity of vision of the turnaround heads is compelling and has been a salutary lesson to me.

Their stress on accountability, for example, prompts me to the realization that in a sophisticated, established school environment it is quite possible to duck personal responsibility. A public school with its tradition of the 'gentleman volunteer' can reap benefit from the generous commitment of many of its staff, but in that rather fuzzy culture it is relatively easy to pass the buck. Committee structures, much favoured at Eton for example, are good for involving people and airing views, but cannot have the crisp focus of an accountable individual.

There is a balance to be struck. The broadly collegial atmosphere of a boarding school is something I treasure. In a culture where there is a degree of professional licence and people are prepared to be flexible, and where regulation and direction are tempered by common sense, teachers flourish. They are more prepared to take the initiative and deal with situations without prompting and more likely to come up with good ideas than their colleagues who are directed and checked at every stage. Yet in an environment in which people are allowed to get on with things, it is too easy to assume that all are purposeful and that all is well. It is a lesson that has been brought home to me. If juggling is the quintessential skill for a head, then juggling personal autonomy and accountability is the toughest task.

The lesson above all I have learnt, however, is that effective heads are driven by passion. Whatever the well-spring of their motivation, they are carried along by a profound desire to give young people for whom they are responsible the best chances in life. No amount of management-speak and desktop efficiency can turn a school around. The qualities that matter are steadfastness of purpose, energy and belief.

11

Boarding

Why is it in our own country that boarding schools tend to be treated as a kind of lunatic fringe or as peripheral at best? I have had the privilege of travelling abroad and visiting many schools. Wherever I have been around the world, British boarding schools attract at the least fascination and usually admiration. Those parts of the world that trace an historic connection with Britain, from the Indian sub-continent to America, have borrowed extensively from the British tradition of education. Even more strikingly, in those parts of the world that view the British boarding school tradition afresh, there is a huge appetite for what we offer.

We know our schools are a popular choice for those wishing to study here. There are over twenty thousand non-British pupils in schools registered with the Independent Schools Council (ISC) whose parents live overseas, and there are others who have an address in the UK. But the influence is much deeper than that: the ethos and style of British boarding schools have been translated into many countries. What is it that overseas parents and educators perceive?

In part it may be a glimpsing, a take, on an historic ideal burnished by the history of empire and the sheen of historic names. Sometimes indeed, conversation can reveal that we talk at cross purposes. Some years ago when I spoke to a patently enthusiastic audience of educators in the Great Hall of the People in Beijing there was a palpable desire to find out more about British boarding schools. What magic factor might there be that made these schools special and which my hosts might take away the better to enhance their own system in a competitive globalized economy? I spoke at some length about pastoral care. I became aware that there were heads nodding in agreement in the rows in front of me but also some bemused expressions. It was only after some while that I realized my phrase 'pastoral care' was being translated as 'corporal punishment'.

Whatever the misconnections and misunderstandings, there is also respect for the virtues we espouse. These educators working in very different cultures witness the confidence and social competence of the students who have been to our schools. They note that they are multi-faceted and flexible, they see that our students are confident individuals and that they understand something about community. Ignorant of political posturing in the UK, they see what we do as a thoroughly good thing.

There have been times though when I have felt that boarding in Britain is in a tailspin. After all, there are some 40 per cent fewer boarding-school places than 20 years ago.

While numbers have risen slightly, in historic terms, the 68,000 pupils currently in independent boarding schools (there are an additional 5,000 in state boarding schools) is a low level. Even within the independent school sector, boarding, which was once the defining characteristic of the great British liberal tradition of the public school, comprises only 13 per cent of pupils in ISC schools. For a variety of reasons, parents have turned their faces away from boarding schools.

From the 1960s onwards there developed a view that sending a child to a boarding school was somehow 'unnatural', that it perverted family relationships and abrogated responsibility for a child to people who run shadowy, strange institutions. And, in truth, boarding schools were in part to blame. For all that there were exciting schools with committed, outstanding teach-ers, there was also complacency, self-indulgence and a remarkable lack of accountability. There are many men and women who speak warmly of their boarding-school experience in the 1960s, but there are also casualties. I meet them: people who were scarred by the experience and who needed therapy of one kind or another, not least writing about their experiences, in order, as the phrase now has it, to 'move on'. The fall-out from the exposure of Jimmy Savile and the Yewtree enquiry has revealed shocking betrayals of trust in a variety of contexts, including boarding schools. In some ways more revealing has been how pervasive was the culture of the 1970s and 80s that ignored threats to young people and sometimes accepted behaviour by adults that we now see as abusive.

The Children Act of 1989 and ensuing legislation has prompted a sea change in attitudes and practice. The Act is principally concerned with local authority responsibilities for child protection, but it clearly states that children's welfare should be the paramount concern of the courts and also specifies that any delay in the system's processes has a detrimental effect on the child. Subsequent legislation concerning the inspection of schools has extended the view that it is the interests of the child that should come first. By making it an *obligation* on heads to follow up every concern, query and allegation, issues that once were hidden in the half-light are now subject to the full glare of a spotlight. In truth, this legislation and the change in attitude it has prompted has been a godsend to schools, and especially to boarding schools.

In recent years we have considered ourselves fortunate at Eton in having a good working relationship with our local social services. The trust that grows from sound professionalism is such that all concerns about child welfare, current or historic, are logged and discussed with them in the knowledge that such conversations will not automatically lead to the nuclear option with police cars parked in front of family homes. A sound, open, professional relationship between social services and the school is likely to provide the best support for young people. Looking back over my time in schools, it is clear to me that it is only in the last ten years or so that schools which have developed this kind of good, professional relationship can make the case for boarding as modern, outward-looking, professionally run and safe.

Another factor playing on the minds of parents has been social class, accompanied by its neighbour, privilege. For many people, boarding schools are still viewed as bastions of privilege and there is no denying that there was a time in our nation's history when such schools liked to see themselves as set apart, removed from the lives of fellow citizens. There are times when it still feels as though a deadly cloud of class awareness hangs over boarding schools. Yet the times are changing. Many schools now see virtue in creating a community with a range of characters, backgrounds and skills. In part this has been driven by a changing market, but it is more than that. One of boarding's strengths is enabling young people to learn to live with different types of people. A healthy mix of young people of different social background, ethnicity and interests is beneficial to all. In a way not seen in the past, many heads and governing bodies actively pursue this ideal.

I am only too aware that lazy assumptions can lead to sloppy journalism. Eton has, for some journalists, the convenience of being a four-letter word and is often used as a generic term. An angry correspondent writes to condemn me for sending boys sick with the disease SARS to recuperate on the Isle of Wight. This is news to me, until I discover that a reporter has described a school unknown to me as 'Eton' in his article. In the same way the phrase 'boarding school' can be used to describe a set of attitudes that have little to do with a school's daily life.

Cardboard cut-outs suit some politically motivated opinion-formers, whose nervousness about the 'class thing' may have been one reason for the decline in boarding numbers over the past 20 years, but a more obvious reason has been the sheer cost of it all. The need to develop and maintain top-line facilities, offer competitive rates of pay to staff and withstand the constant waves of expensive bureaucracy have proved a lethal cocktail. Escalating costs have further removed whole groups of families who might otherwise see a boarding education as right for their sons and daughters. When I started teaching at Tonbridge in the 1970s, the head master, Christopher Everett, was wont to use country GPs, senior policemen and airline pilots as his benchmark. Comparing their salary with school fees he would reckon that they would be able to afford to have two children at boarding school. The average senior boarding school fee has risen dramatically over the past four decades and annually by 1% more than inflation since the economic crisis of 2008. For a family with two or more children paying out of earned income, finding money for boarding fees has become a very tall order.

Furthermore, governments have withdrawn their support: the funding of boarding places for young people from difficult backgrounds who might benefit from boarding largely dried up in the 1980s. At just the time when the government could have injected more money into boarding places, a flawed Assisted Places scheme for day places was introduced. It was flawed because it was misdirected. With assessments of financial need based on income and not wealth it proved too easy to play the system. Self-employed business people could show that they had no income despite their assets. There were even examples of parents borrowing a tatty car to come to interview. The scheme worked well for some families, but too seldom did it reach out to those who were in most need of help. An additional issue was the focus on day places, which had the effect in some areas of setting independent and state schools against each other in competition for pupils, thereby exacerbating tensions.

In recent times there have been signs of a shift of opinion in political circles. Successive governments have stated a qualified belief in the effectiveness of boarding for young people. Some new academies have met with approval for including a limited amount of boarding provision. However, these are hesitant, initial steps. Boarding in the UK still faces significant challenges.

First, the ever-rising costs will continue to be a challenge for boarding schools. They are expensive places to run. Many boarding schools have made great efforts to bear down on inflationary pressures, but the pressure is constant. Some schools try to offer too much. There is a place for a good boarding experience focused on a limited choice of options (of academic subject, sport or other activity) which can be made more affordable to more people. In this context the facilities arms race must surely cease. In truth, some of these facilities have proved to be a passing fad. I remember in the early 1990s that something called CDT was all the rage. Craft, design and technology centres were the thing, but design and technology have undergone several iterations since then. There are purpose-built CDT mausoleums now used for other projects.

A more significant challenge, however, I suspect, will be managing and shaping parents' aspirations and expectations. It is a fact that some of the more traditional boarding-school parents, parents who have often intuitively understood the philosophy of boarding, can no longer entertain the idea of educating their children along those lines. Many boarding schools have responded by significantly increasing their bursary pots to support a range of family incomes: indeed, in 2009 one pupil in four at ISC schools received scholarships or bursaries from their school. This has led to more of a social mix in our schools, a mix that is the greater because the full-fee-paying parents who have taken the places of some more traditional families are a more diverse collection than in the 1970s, with a wider range of aspirations and perceptions of what a boarding school means. This can be stimulating and refreshing. But some traditional assumptions about boarding schools – for example, that there is innate value in an all-round education or attendance at chapel or, indeed, that rules should be applied consistently to all pupils – are not necessarily shared and are sometimes challenged robustly by parents. Boarding schools have to state more clearly what they believe is important. Understandably, some parents buying an expensive boarding product for the first time expect an entirely bespoke service, shaped exactly to their requirements.

Many parents increasingly operate in a changing and uncertain business and professional world. They pay substantial sums of money for their child's boarding education and while many will look to the long-term benefits for a happy and developing child, a number will look for immediate tangible returns on their investment in terms of exam grades and a place at a prestigious university. At times the pressure parents put on schools is little short of harassment and can cause some heads to respond with ready short-term solutions which may lead to longer-term problems; for example, feeling impelled to focus more intently on exam grades, or even, in some cases, distorting disciplinary processes for a quiet life. Parents are, in one sense, customers and pay a lot of money, but they should not, idcally, be paying at a go-as-you-please counter of unrelated choices. These days boarding schools are highly professional institutions; parents are paying for professional expertise. Sometimes they need to be reminded. In particular, parents need to be fully aware that they are not just buying a product but buying into a philosophy.

There are, in my view, two fundamental truths to school life:

1. Young people learn at least as much outside the classroom as in it.

2. Young people learn more from each other than they do from adults.

Great teachers and great schools create the environment in which these things happen. As a society we have rather lost sight of these central truths, which apply to every type of school, be it day, boarding, private or state. We prefer instead to believe that management is a more efficient alternative to nurturing relationships. A top-down approach lacks roots; schools cannot grow and flourish. Throw into the mix our national obsession with data measurement, which segments and fragments the breadth of learning, and we risk undermining the subtlety and complexity of a child's education. Boarding schools offer an antidote to this creeping disease: they offer organic growth rather than measured atrophy.

The people who tend this growth are the teachers. Teaching is a noble profession. Teachers devote their energy and skill to helping the young develop into purposeful adults who, in their turn, may lead and change society for the better. On a wet Wednesday when a class is playing up, a teacher may not feel that this is the case, but this noble vision is at the heart of it. Most teachers have a strong belief in their purpose and they are the most important resource for any school.

If you agree that a school's most important resource is indeed its teachers you will want young people to have as much contact with them as possible. In a day school, typically, there will be around thirty-five hours of possible contact time each week and at secondary level, unlike primary school, that contact will be split among a number of teachers. Parents whose children are in transition to secondary school are often struck by the lack of personal knowledge teachers have of their children.

In a typical boarding school there will be double that amount of contact time – and that excludes the weekend. Boarders have the focused attention of adults, particularly in their boarding houses, who are committed to a cause. What the experience of boarding school life shows is that a virtuous circle is created when time, real time, is given to the nurturing of relationships – pupil to pupil, adult to pupil and, just as importantly, adult to adult: pupils need to see adults getting along well or at least working together effectively. From these relationships everything that is valuable and long-lasting will grow: and this flows from the vocational commitment of well-chosen and well-trained staff. In the jargon phrase, the 'social capital' the young people develop is substantial and on a sure foundation. For families where parents lead busy lives, or where there is no family structure at home, or simply where there is an understanding of the value of this approach, this level of attention is powerful and pontentially transformative for the child.

The boarding housemaster or housemistress is the central figure in the school lives of our young people. We look for exceptional people prepared to give of themselves throughout the week, people who choose to live the life rather than simply do a job. Great Schools are fashioned from great commitment. I have always worked on the principle that housemasters should be teachers who are also actively engaged in the full school programme as well as having their particular pastoral responsibilities. There are UK boarding schools that operate a successful, non-academic house parent model, but I believe that the direct engagement of the housemaster or mistress in the fullness of pupils' school life has a profound influence on the young, offers a living role model and can lead to better relationships.

A few years ago Eton was paid a visit by some people about to open a boarding school in the Far East. They spent a great deal of time looking at Eton's boarding structure and philosophy. When their new school opened, we discovered that their first decision had been to appoint one group of people to teach academic subjects and an entirely different group to run the boarding houses. At a stroke they had set their school on a different path. Even by Western standards, the British commitment to pastoral care stands unique: visiting one of the top American boarding schools, I was struck by their arrangement that the people who live in with pupils are young teachers who work their passage over a few years in order to 'earn' a nice staff house down the hill away from the children. Our expectation that the housemaster/mistress should be an experienced teacher completely engaged in the lives of their pupils is a hugely valuable and distinctive part of the British tradition.

When it comes to creating a compelling, supportive culture, boarding schools have a distinct advantage: they offer a range and breadth many day schools find hard to achieve. Rather than an academic curriculum with some extracurricular activities bolted on – a model seen in many day schools – good boarding schools believe in a genuinely holistic approach which sees the curriculum as a totality: an educational philosophy in which sport, music, art, drama and many other activities are seen as being of a piece with moral, social and intellectual development. The timetable reflects this philosophy, creating long periods of time for pupils outside the classroom. The traditional model operates with three full and three half teaching days in a six-day week, with half-days for sports practice, rehearsals and downtime. Even the full days tend to operate with space for non-classroom activity: in the winter, for example, afternoon lessons may start at dusk, thus using the light to best effect outdoors.

It is not a question of dictating pupils' behaviour, but creating a culture in which young people will develop themselves. In their houses, in lessons, in a host of other activities, boarders often learn a level of social skills far in advance of their years. They learn to mix, to tolerate each other, to appreciate the strengths of someone of a very different nature, to get the best out of each other.

Teenagers tend to be clannish. Intuitively they get on very well with those who are like-minded. Boarders learn to get on with those they don't initially like. It has been one of the delights of my boarding experience to see the apparent misfit become accepted as part of a group and, in time, celebrated for his quirky individuality. A case in point was the 13-year-old who arrived at Eton with his sewing machine: at 18 he triumphantly held a cat-walk fashion show in school for which he made the clothes for both his male and female models.

While the political climate seems a little warmer about the educational benefit of boarding, there is a tendency in some quarters to see provision only as a stop-gap means to arrest some deep social problems. Boarding schools, independent and state, have indeed shown themselves to be successful in offering a way forward for vulnerable children from complex family backgrounds. The evidence now increasingly demonstrates that boarding, in both the independent and state sectors, achieves demonstrable results. An analysis of 'assisted boarding' (where young people are given financial support to enable them to board) has shown that assisted boarders achieve more and go further than their counterparts. One example is Norfolk County Council's Assisted Boarding Project, in conjunction with the Royal National Children's Foundation, which placed 31 vulnerable young people aged 7–18 into nine boarding schools, with strong educational results; it produced good value for money, too, comparing the annual cost of taking a child into care (£46,000) with boarding school fees of between £10,000–£30,000. At the top end of academic league tables, boarding schools like Eton, Wycombe Abbey and Winchester compete with academically highly selective day schools, depending on which league table you choose to follow.

However, the real virtue of a boarding-school education is above and beyond academic attainment. The genius of good boarding schools is that they offer an answer to contemporary concerns about social cohesion. With their capacity to bring people together and create supportive and resilient communities, boarding schools are more relevant now than at any other period in my lifetime. They are effective. They work.

Boarding works best for young people from difficult backgrounds, however, when they are part of an integrated and varied community. We need outstanding environments in which young people learn from each other how to become useful and purposeful citizens. Many more young people would have their life chances dramatically enhanced if they were offered the chance of a boarding education, but if boarding is seen as a quick fix for social ills, everyone suffers.

British boarding schools are at their best as places whose culture supports and challenges children and helps develop true self-esteem, where the teachers go the extra mile without question, where individuality is celebrated, where children achieve things they would not have believed possible.

So there is good reason to be positive about boarding. The philosophy of British boarding schools is relevant to the needs of modern society: it achieves results, it gives wonderful opportunities for our young people and is viewed as world-class by people around the globe. They are a significant national asset, a unique environment in which British and overseas students, both fee-paying and financially supported, can live and work together to the benefit of society. We need to use this asset. As things stand, we are wasting a wonderful opportunity. We need government to renew commitment to state boarding schools, increase the number of places available and introduce a new-style government-funded Assisted Places scheme in independent schools focused squarely on boarding need.

Initiatives such as these will open up access to an educational sector of world class to those who need most help. This will cost money in difficult economic times, but in social terms it would be cost-effective. It would be money well spent and all members of the boarding-school family, including well-established boarding schools like Eton, should play an active part.

Holyport College: a new state boarding school

It was a belief in the transformative capacity of a good boarding culture that led Eton College to take the decision to sponsor and support a new state boarding school, Holyport College. We wanted something of the experience of being in a boarding school to be more available to more people. Holyport was created using the mechanism of the free school movement, giving the freedom to structure a school in ways different from the template. There was, we discovered, no real understanding of boarding in officialdom – that children would need beds, for example, was initially something of a revelation.

The proposition is simple. State boarding schools are mostly comprehensive in intake, and are funded in much the same way as any other day school. Parents pay for the boarding element with the government capping the amount that can be charged. In 2014 the average fee charged to parents was some £11,500 per annum, a sum that is just about one-third of the fee for the most expensive independent boarding schools. The ethos and philosophy of a boarding education thus become available to a much wider range of parents and children. For working parents who see the social and cultural benefits of boarding but who cannot afford the very high fees of the independents, state boarding schools are an attractive option.

There is, naturally enough, considerable variety among state boarding schools. Some offer hostel-style residential accommodation to a minority (sometimes a small minority) of pupils in what is fundamentally a day school. At the other end, a school like Wymondham College in Norfolk has some 650 boarders in its school population of 1,300, making it one of the larger boarding school anywhere. Notwithstanding its mix of day and boarding students, the school is run and feels like a boarding school, with a clear emphasis on pastoral care and a range of activities.

At present, the option of state boarding is limited to a small number of schools across the country. There should be many more. The tradition, expertise, and cultural support embodied by world-class British boarding schools are too significant and beneficial to young people to allow them to be the preserve of a select few.

After a great deal of persistence and hard work by a team including senior people from Eton College, Holyport opened in September 2014 as a mixed-ability comprehensive school with roughly half day students and half boarding. Boarders have an all-embracing experience and day students are in school until at least 5.30 p.m. each day. The local authority has responsibility for admission to day places according to its own policies; boarders are selected by the school, but only insofar as they are 'suitable to board'. There is a good mix of students: children from fee-paying prep schools live and work with children from poorer families who are eligible for pupil premium or with children in care whose boarding fees are paid for by a local authority. A great range of young people can benefit from this arrangement. What is crucial, however, is that the ethos of the boarding part of the school should reflect that of a stable, aspirational family. This statement may sound rather blunt, but it is logical. The kind of effective modern boarding about which I feel so strongly only works well when the rhythm and dynamic of the group is positive – children from less advantaged backgrounds can be swept along by it and young people from all backgrounds benefit. Boarding institutions that become drop zones for young people with problems develop a very different atmosphere. Holyport is not designed to be a special school, but a very good mainstream state boarding school.

Eton's relationship with Holyport is intended to be visible and meaningful, and to have an impact over the long term. Initially the experience of senior staff, both operational and strategic, has helped give shape to the school's vision of itself, its detailed policies and, crucially, the appointment of its leaders. It was not intended that Eton's involvement would be a financial one but Eton has helped out where no funds have been available; for example, building a multi-use games area (with help from the Old Etonian Association). More significant is the commitment to form direct departmental relationships responding to particular needs. These vary from teaching Latin to special workshops in a variety of subjects.

There are many ways in which the two schools are further developing relationships: Eton's sixth-formers, for example, volunteer to mentor young pupils during evening prep time. I have been struck by the willingness of teachers and students in both schools to connect. In some ways this experience has been salutary: there is such appetite among many teachers and parents for links that enable all our young people to develop. These connections cannot be forced, and must be based on trust, which takes time to build. This is not an area in which government diktat is likely to be productive: encouragement and example show the way ahead.

It would be a major step forward if leading independent boarding schools and government took a decision together to concentrate on the benefits of boarding. An expansion of boarding places through state boarding schools would be popular with many parents and in the long run it would also be cost-effective. It would dramatically improve the life chances of young people from disadvantaged backgrounds and would play to a distinctive national strength in education.

12

Co-Ed or Not Co-Ed?

I have worked variously in all-boys' schools, the rather strange hybrid that is a boys' school with girls in the sixth form, and in full co-education. I am struck by the laboured way advocates of different systems stress the virtue of their particular way of doing things as though, by definition, co-education or a single-sex approach are intrinsically marks of excellence. I have visited outstanding co-educational and single-sex schools and also some spectacularly bad ones of both persuasions. What makes a good school is so much more than its organization by gender. It is still the case, however, that some proponents on both sides engage in a bleating mantra of the Orwellian 'four legs good, two legs bad' variety. Shrill advocates of single-sex will make ever bolder claims, while the co-education lobby, now so strongly in the ascendant, blithely disregard criticism of the status quo.

Looking back over the last quarter of a century, it is striking to see how the landscape has developed. In the independent school world single-sex schools have in large numbers converted to some sort of co-education. When I became a member of HMC (the Headmasters' Conference) in 1989, it was in the main a gentleman's club for the heads of boys' schools: of the 240 members at the time, only some 40 were from co-ed schools. Indeed, this band of co-ed heads felt beleaguered, not least when the advent of national league tables revealed single-sex schools at the top of the tree, sufficiently so to organize themselves into a special interest group offering mutual support and a forum in which to fashion an apologia for co-education. Today that situation is rather neatly reversed: the number of boys' schools in HMC is 40.

This is not a phenomenon to be found just in UK independent schools. The latter part of the twentieth century saw the inexorable rise of co-education in schools across the world. In some cases this was the result of robust action: the Americans imposed co-education on the Japanese after the Second World War in order to break away from the military mentality of boys' academies. In some cases co-education has been seen as a panacea: in parts of India the introduction of co-education is viewed as an answer to problems of pupil discipline. In rather more cases, the move to co-education has been a consequence of simple economics, a logical way to fill empty places as has happened in UK independent schools over the past 30 years. In the main, however, from Bristol to Beijing, from Düsseldorf to Delhi, co-education is a social vision and has seemed the natural, obvious and right way.

The history of education had given a bad deal to girls, with the odds stacked against them for generations. Training for domestic life should take place in the home; the institution of the school was a male business. Well into the Victorian age, the assumption remained that education for girls should be practical and social, not intellectual. Some of them might attend local day schools for a few years, but only a very small number attended expensive, fashionable boarding schools with a non-academic curriculum. In the UK, it was not until 1850 that the redoubtable Frances Mary Buss established the North London Collegiate School offering a similar education at a high level to that given to boys. Other institutions were founded, such as the Girls Public Day School Company in 1872, subsequently called the GPD Trust, to create further opportunities for girls, but at the dawn of the twentieth century less than a quarter of all girls attended any school at all. In the independent sector, the girls' schools that did exist, even those inspired by remarkable pioneers, tended to be overshadowed by boys' schools with their long-standing foundations and relative wealth. What else would one expect when the broadly held view lingered that boys needed formal education for the world of work while girls, in effect, needed to be educated to support them. Whatever other motivations lay behind the mass exodus away from single-sex schools, co-education was about giving a helping hand to girls.

How times have changed! The growing clamour in the twenty-first century has been to find ways to support boys who now significantly underperform girls in almost every level of school assessment. Indeed, contemporary newspapers are peppered with laments along the lines: 'Is there anything good about men?' So was co-education a good idea that has just gone too far? Is there something to be said for acknowledging differences of gender, or does the equality agenda trump all other cards? It is worth investigating the principal claims.

Advocates of co-education often cite Plato for historic gravitas. Plato certainly saw virtue in boys and girls being educated in many of the same things, but was less evidently a proponent of co-education as described in modern schools. He can be presented, though, as the path to a philosophical 'truth' of the sublime logic of co-education.

For hundreds of years, however, this approach did not seem logical at all. Men and women were seen to have different roles and functions in society and needed to be educated in very different ways. While there is some evidence that boys and girls were taught together, at least for part of the time, as far back as the Middle Ages, it was not until 1818 and the founding of the Dollar Academy that parents had the choice of a co-educational secondary school for their children. In the nineteenth century such schools were few and far between. Ask most people of the time what they imagined a school to be and it would have been an institution for boys with, perhaps, an alternative provision for girls. This orthodoxy was really only broken apart 50 years ago and in a remarkably short time has, in turn, become the new orthodoxy.

Educated, as I was, in what some see as the antediluvian world of the boys' boarding school, and given my early teaching career in the same vein, it was not until I made the conscious decision to experience co-ed in my second headship at Oakham School that I had the opportunity to test some of these claims at first hand.

Before moving to Oakham I had experience of teaching girls, but only in the sixth form. I had found it an unsatisfactory arrangement. Entering a boys' school for the sixth-form years took a girl of considerable strength of will, or worse, a simpering willingness to play up to adolescent perceptions about women, for her time to be successful or happy. There were some girls who had a great time, but there were also sad casualties, girls whose self-confidence was shot to pieces. It is not an experience I would have wished for my daughter. I felt at the time that choice was a good thing for families, that different arrangements would suit different boys and girls but that the choice should be between distinctive approaches and philosophies, not a cobbled-together patchwork – it should be between either single-sex or genuine co-ed. Even today there are half-hearted independent schools that still remain, in effect, boys' schools that have admitted girls. As I was to discover, genuine co-ed is a different proposition.

And so to Oakham. It was, and is, a remarkable school in a number of ways, not least in being the first boys' school to transform itself utterly by making the move to full co-education in 1970. For a variety of reasons, local government prompted the school to change direction: continuing in the same old way was no longer viable. A visionary and forceful headmaster, John Buchanan, turned a rather down-at-heel, second-rate local boarding school of fewer than four hundred boys into a boarding and day school of over one thousand pupils, half boys and half girls, drawn from across the country and abroad. It stands as a remarkable success story. The dramatic momentum of change was achieved in only ten hectic and exciting years, though long-standing staff recognized that it took twice that time for the school to become wholly comfortable with the habits and mentality of a genuine co-ed school. In part this lengthy period of transition was necessary in order to create the facilities that allowed equal opportunities for boys and girls, in sport, for example. More significant, however, was the time it took for a generation of (mostly male) teachers, used to a particular atmosphere and style, to adapt – or leave.

Converting a school from single-sex to co-ed, or vice versa, is not a matter of flicking a switch, of making a few logistical adjustments to the lavatories and find-ing a compatible school uniform. They offer different experiences and require a different approach from teachers. Oakham was a mature and successful co-ed school by the time of my arrival. Its strength was offering similar opportunities for achievement and self-esteem to both boys and girls while celebrating their difference. So, competitive team sport for girls was strongly encouraged, as was boys' participation in music and drama. Great play was made of activities in which both boys and girls equally could share recognition: the Duke of Edinburgh Award was held in high regard throughout the school with over one thousand boys and girls reaching their Gold Awards, pursuing very similar paths.

What struck me, as a new arrival in 1996, was that Oakham passed the test of authenticity. It felt as though it knew what it was – a healthy and balanced community for boys and girls. This is the ultimate test for prospective parents. Whatever the prospectus-speak, does the school feel right? In the end a decision on choice of school is made on a reaction as much visceral as reasoned. Statistics and rhetoric can be bewildering; instinct is a surer guide.

The principal claims made by the co-ed camp are that boys and girls are more likely to be confident expressing opinions in front of each other and, indeed, more likely to be more respectful of one other. In sum, they find it easier to make real friends with the opposite sex. All this leads, the argument goes, to greater adaptability in the workplace and to a more balanced adult life. There is certainly some truth in the proposition, but it is all too easy to make sweeping statements.

I have seen sound and long-lasting friendships blossom in co-ed environments, though this is more evident at sixth-form age. In the middle teenage years, it is a common sight in a good co-ed school to see boys and girls choose to sit in gender groups, in a classroom or dining hall. As head of a co-ed school I was relaxed about that: nature finds its own way and need not be forced.

It is true, too, that the behaviour of groups of boys and girls can be positively influenced by each other. While the notion that girls 'civilize' boys has developed into something of an urban myth, there are everyday moments that show adolescent boys as just a little less unthinking and boorish than they might have been. And it can work the other way around. At Oakham I overheard a sharp-tongued series of verbal assaults in a neighbouring room as a group of 15-year-old girls went for each other, into which maelstrom wandered a boy of their own age who mumbled, 'What's the problem then?' – and all was peace.

But, as so often, it is easy to overstate the case. I have seen both boys and girls just as disconnected and unsure in a co-ed as in a single-sex school. Whether it is the 13-year-old boy taunting 'unclean' girls about their periods or girls publicly ridiculing the nerdy, uncool boy, adolescence is a testing time in whatever environment. What matters is the school culture created and reaffirmed day by day, where there are good role models and where parameters of acceptable behaviour are clearly drawn and, more importantly, clearly understood.

Boys' schools, at least the thoughtful, modern type that are not shackled to stereotypes, tend to believe that boys gain confidence in their ability to learn without being compared with girls, who mature more quickly and who tend to enjoy more success in school. For some boys, the release from the added pressure of constant comparison with girls' performance can be a boon. Enabling a son to have his place in the light away from the shining achievement of his sister is a regular refrain in my conversations with parents. Boys can grow at their own pace and 'be boys' for as long as they need, protected from social pressures to be involved with girls before they are ready. Some heads of boys' schools will speak of freedom from distractions, so boys do not need to waste energy posturing or trying to live up to the gender stereotypes so routinely thrown at young people by media and society at large; their focus can be on their own achievements – and they can celebrate as boys together.

For some people, the shadow of *Tom Brown's School Days* lingers, with images of unbridled testosterone, of driving competitiveness and insensitive self-assertion. Good, modern boys' schools, their advocates say, make a virtue of positive male role models and create a culture which promotes respect for the many ways to be a man and which explores sensitive gender and sex-related issues. This I have certainly witnessed. The truth, however, is that the range of quality and philosophy in boys' schools is vast. At their worst, they can incubate selfishness and allow a monolithic view of manhood. At their best they encourage boys to become grounded, positive young men able to identify and celebrate difference.

The arguments in favour of girls' schools run on similar lines. In the UK, the Girls' Schools Association stresses the differing rates of maturity between boys and girls, the potential for girls to have greater self-confidence in the impressionable middle teen years, the breadth of opportunity unfettered by stereotypes – all of which are arguments deployed by boys' schools. Advocates for girls' schools, however, tend to claim notable gains in academic performance and university entrance. Here the evidence is debatable. It is true that single-sex schools traditionally dominate league tables, but that is a consequence of the historic traditions of well-established, academically selective metropolitan schools: there just is no co-ed equivalent of St Paul's Boys and St Paul's Girls in London. The temptation to trenchant advocacy does not advance the case for single-sex education.

Where girls' schools do have a very good case, however, is presenting themselves as specialists in the education of girls, understanding how girls' friendships shift and change, how they can support each other effectively and how they can be encouraged to become more resilient in an environment in which some of the sharp edges of social pressure are removed.

If the battle lines of rhetoric are clearly drawn, what is the evidence one way or the other? One of the significant changes to the gender argument has been our better understanding of the way the brain works. In the 1960s and 70s, the idea gained currency that gender is largely a social construct and that gender bias can be reduced, even erased, by effective co-education. This has given way to a more nuanced view. Teachers now have access to greater knowledge about the way young people respond at different parts of their lives and why they do so. The question thrown up by any number of research projects in recent years is whether, if at all, gender differences are hardwired.

Before the science came the journalism. With a canny eye to popular sentiment, John Gray scored a major publicity triumph with his 1992 book *Men are from Mars, Women are from Venus* in which he purported to chart the gulf between men and women. It is a theme that has reverberated around the Western world, spawning an industry in its wake.

To the voice of the popular sage is added the work of a growing tribe of neuroscientists and psychologists such as Louann Brizendine and Leonard Sax. While the momentum of their research drives us to believe that verbal agility and psychic abilities are inherent in the structure of the female brain and that crisp problem-solving is an attribute of the male, one is left with the feeling that this work tends to find support for generalizations that have already become part of popular myth. It is based on observation, certainly, but observation that is yanked into a position to define a case. Take Leonard Sax and his claim that boys and girls actually need different classroom temperatures in which to function properly. Most teachers would observe that boys are dozier than girls in warm rooms, girls more ready to complain when a room is cooler, but to elevate the distinction to a six-degree rule is a neuro-leap too far.

Repetition of words like 'hardwired' or 'innate' describes a clarity which is not substantiated. Emphatic overstatement risks denigrating some significant advances. We know more fully, for example, how the brain connects as it grows and at what ages the key connections take place, further illustrating the extent to which boys and girls develop at different rates – the labyrinthine path to maturity.

The thrust of neuroscientific research demonstrates there are *some* natural differences that are relevant when considering schooling, but not so significant as to determine the choice of schooling by gender. Given that the brain changes throughout one's lifetime and, arguably, that differences by gender in adults are as marked as in adolescent children and teenagers, the 'nature card' in itself is not enough. The power of nurture on our young people is as strong a contributor to the healthy growth of boys and girls.

In my own professional life, I have experienced different styles and approaches to schooling, including arrangement by gender. I was attracted to Oakham School because I knew it to be one of the most effective independent co-educational schools in the country. It was a delight. Boys and girls were treated even-handedly. They had equal opportunities and learnt to have friends of both genders. It was, broadly, a happy place: the kind of school you would like to have your child educated in (and I did). So it was with some trepidation that I returned to an all-boys' school, at Eton.

It is, as any woman would observe, a very male place. The attitude of some boys towards girls is arguably less mature than in a co-ed setting and there is a competitive drive which could become unhealthy. I was surprised, however, to discover benefits – and not where I might have expected them.

It is true at a selective boys' school that standards of sporting and academic achievement are very high, but I suspect the effects of being in a boys' school are marginal. There is a ready assumption that it is the boys' school that stands up for manly challenges, such as rugby. Yet rugby at co-ed Oakham was of greater significance to the life of the whole school than at Eton: hundreds of spectators, at least as many girls as boys, would watch the 1st XV. It is also true that in some respects a boys' school removes some hidden constraints on choice – the take-up of subjects such as English and Modern Languages in a boys' school tends to be higher than among boys in a co-ed, for example.

What really struck me, however, is the pleasure boys have simply being boys together, whether it is a casual game of football or mucking about with friends, able to develop bonds of friendship without worrying how it looks through the prism of male/female relationships. I had forgotten, too, how liberating it is for a boy to play in an orchestra where all the violins are played by boys (rather than the traditional model in which violins are mostly played by girls and the sounding brass by boys). I was surprised to see just how powerful single-sex drama can be when there is trust. I have seen boys playing intimately across gender and exploring emotion. It struck me that there is a quality and depth of cultural experience that would be unlikely in front of an audience of their co-educational peers. Early on at Eton, I watched a studio production of a play by boys that involved on-stage intimacy between male and female characters. It was performed delicately and without embarrassment. More remarkable to me was the accepting response of the boy audience: they saw the relationship and drama in its own terms, not a wolf-whistle or whispered leer to be heard.

I have always held to the view that teaching is teaching and a half-decent practitioner will respond to the needs of pupils as individually as possible, whoever they are. In any event, the range of difference and need within a group of boys or a group of girls in themselves can be considerable. Putting boys and girls together simply adds to the range of difference. Responding to pupils individually is a good place for any aspiring teacher to start, but as my experience has grown I have come more to the recognition that on balance there are things that can be achieved with a single-sex group, especially in the middle teenage years, that are harder to achieve with a mixed group.

In the end, as it should be, the choice of the school is a matter for parents. Parents will juggle many considerations and, while I would not advise that being co-educational or single-sex should be a determining factor, how the school enables boys to be boys and girls to be girls would be high on my list. Above all, apply the authenticity test: does the school feel comfortable in its own skin?

13

'Doing the Job'

It is never easy being honest about personal motivation. Being the head of a school for a period of time can be an isolating experience; heads seek to be friendly with members of the school community but cannot develop real friendships. The person with whom the buck stops must be seen to be somewhat removed, passionate about his school but dispassionate when it comes to people and events. Given the pressure, the public scrutiny and the vulnerability of the job, it is surprising anyone wants to do it. The art of removing an unwanted head has been practised and honed in the independent sector over many years, but in a measurement age state heads can find their tenure abruptly truncated. The language of football managership is frequently heard. Who will be the first to go this season?

There are times when I have felt that my prime motivation is a Yeatsian 'lonely impulse of delight', taking pleasure, as if at a distance, in the good things being achieved by others, but motivation tends to be many-layered. Feeling useful, exercising a temporary and limited power, being at the centre of things, are probably all in there somewhere. Looking at heads I respect, however, it is striking how many share a sense of their leadership as service. It is an old-fashioned concept, perhaps, and one with religious overtones, yet it is evident in their working lives. These men and women take on an often onerous job because they want to serve young people by enhancing and even transforming their opportunities in life. They have not taken up headship for the money or status, they are not the lead functionaries in a system, nor chief executives, and it can be helpful for parents to bear that in mind when in conversation with them, especially over difficult matters. Being told by a parent, for example, that one 'runs/does not run a good business' is an alien language.

What a head does have to do, however, is deal with a wide range of people and issues. As a young teacher I would sometimes wonder, as I moved smartly from one activity to another in a busy day, quite what the head did. He was always in his study it seemed (at least he was when I went to see him) and was the natural focus for grumbles and criticism. He did not seem to *do* very much at all, certainly by comparison with my daily workload. Most of my colleagues knew, and some said, that they could do a better job. This was odd in one respect because we had no idea really what the job was. In particular, we had little understanding that the essential requirement of a head is the ability to be a decent juggler while retaining a steadfast view about the purpose and direction of the school.

When my turn came, the biggest surprise was that dealing with boys and girls was the easy part. Teenagers can do stupid things, but almost always the situation can be redeemed in some way. The machinations of the adult world are altogether trickier. While teenagers are the point and purpose of the job, this chapter, inevitably, is mostly about adults.

In the week before my first term as a new head, three events in quick succession set the tone. On my desk was a letter from my predecessor to a head of department saying that he should be sacked but it was a matter for the new head. A knock on the door heralded a bitter complaint from a female teacher about the chaplain, a married man who was having an affair she alleged with another female teacher (I was naive enough not to realize straight away that her passion was driven by her own close relationship with the chaplain). Then a phone call brought news that a 14-year-old pupil had killed himself. His funeral, attended by many pupils, took place on the first day of the school year, from which they returned to be addressed by the new head in his first assembly.

A week later an entire lavatory block was smashed, with broken porcelain littered across the yard and on the walls the painted legend, 'Little – tomorrow your head'. There was a moment when I wondered if this catalogue formed part of a training exercise in unlikely eventualities, but they were all too real and, if unusually compressed in time, typical of the incidents with which heads have to deal.

Teachers

Moments of high drama tend to be just that: moments. Daily life brings the demands of different individuals and groups, or 'constituencies' as they tend to be called. The constituency of teachers is the one on which heads spend most time. With excellent teachers working effectively and following the broad script of the school's narrative, the head's life is pretty straightforward, but even in the best-performing schools sustained harmony does not exist.

Interviews as part of annual review for house masters, heads of department and other teachers take up a significant amount of time and this kind of regular personal contact is important. It is too easy to assume that there is ready conversation with colleagues in the usual run of things when in fact the contact is superficial. Time is also spent with teachers on committees. More than any other school I have known, Eton involves masters in a range of committees on educational, pastoral and financial issues (including the scrutiny of departmental budgets). It is, seen one way, an expensive use of teacher time, but the benefit of 'shop floor' knowledge and the direct engagement of teachers in the development of policy has value.

Perhaps as a consequence of Eton-style committee structure, strategic planning documents have been honed down. Once a year a group of teachers representing all the main committees reviews progress over the past year and sets up targets for the next 12 months. These targets are set in the context of the school's underlying principles, which were discussed by various groups of parents, pupils and old boys and agreed by teachers and the governing body. When we had concluded this exercise we realized, to our surprise, that only one of the five underlying principles was about academic life, the rest were about being a fully rounded human being. In retrospect, that would seem about the right balance. I have found a succinct expression of underlying principles central to the way a school should function: everything the school does should be tested against these basic beliefs. In planning terms, the aim, in the style of Ronald Reagan, was to have a document no longer than one side of A4 paper. We tended to fall long of this aim, but a side or two of closely worded targeted text is of a great deal more practical use than the lengthy 'development plans' commonly expected of schools.

Beneath the orbit of planning and review lies the hubbub of daily interaction. Teaching is an unusual business in the sense that teachers start their professional life as middle managers, responsible on their own for the conduct of their classes. And unlike parts of the business world, they spend relatively little time in a direct professional relationship with senior teachers. Especially among those who have known no world other than the academic, there is a tendency to view all management as suspect and designed to impede the teacher, who is doing the real work. It is, of course, a generalization, but from the head's perspective many teachers seem to have a highly individualized sense of their work and, indeed, of their own importance. Schools advocate the virtue of team playing to pupils, yet ironically it is sometimes their teachers who are the least able or willing to play for the team. In part this is a good thing. I would wish pupils to see teachers as rounded people with their passions and idiosyncrasies, not as a faceless company of men and women, but I expect all teachers to support their school's policies, customs and practices. As with most things, it is a question of judgement. I was taken aback, for example, when an Eton master casually informed me that, while he would uphold the rule about pupils smoking in front of him, he had every intention of smoking in front of them.

In any community, especially one that is residential, politics and rumour are rife. All full-time teachers at Eton live in school accommodation in walking distance from the school. It is a wonderful asset in the running of a boarding school, but it does not take too much imagination to appreciate the sensitivities around allocation of staff housing. It is like the politics of car parking in a day school, but with greater intensity.

As a new head I was given two pieces of advice from old hands about dealing with teachers. 'Never say yes in a corridor', said one: your teacher colleagues will take delight in catching you off guard, prompting you to agree to a decision which you may regret. 'Name six', said the other: when the inevitable visit comes from a teacher claiming that all his colleagues feel that … etc., invite him to give six names; if he can, you are in trouble, but the likelihood is not. It has proved sound advice.

Support staff

A boarding school usually employs more support staff than teachers (in Eton's case over six hundred of them). Many of them are house-based and their range of skills is remarkable: cooks, plumbers, financial clerks, painters, groundsmen, surveyors, secretaries, electricians, lab technicians. With a large estate at Eton including 400 buildings (78 of them listed) general maintenance is a considerable task and with 1,300 boys, each with his own room, there is also a considerable hotel operation to be managed, so the head relies on the quality of the bursar and her team to sustain the efficient operation of the plant. In a boarding school, the influence of a good matron in the pastoral setting is often central to a child's happiness. There are many key support roles.

It is a sad feature of all the schools I have known, however, day and boarding, that the work of support staff can be ignored or regarded as of minor consequence. On occasion, I have heard teachers being unfairly off-hand and downright rude about their support-staff colleagues, yet there is often greater loyalty to the institution and personal commitment from them than from some teachers. Sometimes this loyalty spreads across generations. Visited in my study by an octogenarian ex-laundryman who had worked at Eton as had his father, I was somewhat startled when he asked me if he could stand and sing the Eton boating song, which he did, unaccompanied and including verses to which I, for one, did not know the words. Eton meant a lot to him, he said; he had learnt a lot there, too. He was as much an Etonian as any of the boys. A good school community is squarely focused on the young and their learning, but a really good school community has a bigger vision of itself embracing all those who are involved with it, all of them in their own way learners.

On leaving Oakham, we received an album from the support staff. In it were photographs of all the building works undertaken during our time. It was one of the stranger photographic collections – a picture of a rusty boiler juxtaposed with a shiny new one, for example – but it stands as a testament to the cornucopia of skills that is to be found in schools, and we value it as a tribute to people who really cared about their work and their community.

Parents

In dealing with parents a head is likely to feel that 'all life passes here'. I have been fortunate in working in environments where, for the most part, the parents have been well disposed, supportive and grateful for what the school has done for their children. Many heads will find parents a significant burden, either because they are too much involved in the school (as parent governors with an axe to grind, for example) or, more likely, because they have no involvement at all and compound the difficulties their child is facing.

Even in what might appear to some to be the heady climes of independent schools, there are difficulties. As in schools everywhere, the problems some children exhibit are magnified in their parents, such as the boy bully with a hectoring, aspirational father or the anorexic girl with a demanding, relentless mother. Sometimes meeting a parent reveals a great deal: a feckless, pleasant boy who seemed to have no ability at all to organize himself turned out to have a hyper-organized, pleasant father who controlled every minute of the boy's time at home, so that coming to school was his holiday.

Bullying, or attempted bullying, of the head is a sport for some parents, a reflection of their own character or business life or both. Some boast of it to their friends at dinner parties. Early on at Eton I received an unsolicited visit from a parent who a century ago might have been described as a person of distinction in Society. He gave me a list of the things wrong with the school and then told me my job. He went on to bully his son's house master repeatedly. I am grateful to him in one regard; his behaviour prompted us to devise a training course for masters entitled 'dealing with difficult people', a course that has proved popular ever since.

The realization that swiftly comes to any head is that there are no templates for dealing with parents. The face presented to the world by a well-off upper-middle-class family might mask a corrosive or abusive relationship. Parents in receipt of massive financial support might be among those most critical and demanding. As with their children in school, a head needs to deal with each family circumstance individually.

Two tips I would give to parents embarking on their child's school career are: (1) trust the professionals, (2) always voice a concern. Most schools have been around for some while and have dedicated people whose aim is to help your child get on well with life – work with them. Do not always believe rumour, especially if it comes from your own child, but do not hold back from giving voice to a worry or, if you feel the need, making a complaint. Odd though it may sound I have always been pleased to receive a complaint that is specific and over which I can take action. The abiding frustration is the *sotto voce* half-complaint ('I don't want you to do anything, but … '). It is not altogether productive for a head to hold a conversation with a teacher about whom a parent has voiced criticism when the teacher understandably will ask for details and the head, adjured by the parent not to reveal identity, is uncomfortably restrained: such a meeting ends in a fug. There is a natural reluctance to be seen to make a fuss when your child's future, career or happiness is at stake, but it will be a sorry school indeed that is unable to deal professionally and fairly with a genuine concern. As with any professional trade there will be a degree of back-covering along the line, but a parent should feel that the head always has the interest of the child as the foremost priority. In difficult cases this may not be easy, not least because there is a growing tendency for schools to take legal advice, which invariably tells heads to admit to as little as possible, but even in such cases the head who appears to be standing solely in defence of his institution has crossed the line from vocational school master to front-line manager. The challenge for a head is to be both.

Former pupils

The task for a head, particularly in a well-established independent school, is trickier still when dealing with the constituency of former pupils known in that unique English confection as 'old boys and old girls'. The close bonds of affection with their old school fondly described in Edwardian fiction have weakened in a less institutionally minded age, but passions can still run deep. In my early days of headship, the principal function of old boys seemed to be to chunter about decline – of standards, performance, manners, pretty much everything. One old boy of Chigwell, driving past the school one day, was so enraged at the slovenly, outlandish dress being worn by the pupils, that he pulled over, left his car engine running and stormed into my study to complain. The fact that he had happened upon a charity, non-uniform/fancy dress day only partly mollified him. This anger was not uniquely directed at me. My predecessor at Chigwell had taken the sensible decision to stop the practice of giving free beer at old boys' dinners. The opening line of the first letter he opened on the subject began, 'You, sir, are worse than Hitler.'

At Eton, a highlight was the entry into my study of a finger-jabbing old boy who with some vehemence began with the line, 'You're a socialist who won't rest until you have built a mosque on the school playing fields.' As he developed his theme I felt strangely ennobled; I had certainly never previously been described either as a socialist or a mosque builder. He, of course, purported to be speaking 'for many others'. He may have been right, though he did not name six. His passion was real and while I disagreed on every particular, I respected his passion for his school.

The grumbling about change is as nothing by comparison with moans about admissions to the school. There is a small but vociferous group among the old boys of historic schools that seems to assume entry for their family members is an individual right, like passing on membership of a gentleman's club. The majority of heads will warmly welcome family members of old boys and old girls, not least because they tend to have an intuitive understanding of the ethos of the school, but most heads today will wish for as rich a mix of backgrounds, characters and types as they can attract; diversity makes for a better and healthier school. The change to admissions policy enacted at Eton some 15 years ago has led to ever larger numbers applying from a wider range of schools, thereby achieving something of that rich mix. A consequence is that entry is more competitive and odds are higher for everyone.

The fact that all candidates are treated equally and fairly does not make the pain of rejection any easier to bear. It is tough for a boy from a family with extensive historic connections with a school if he does not gain entry, but it is important that every boy achieving a place knows that he has done so wholly on his own merits. On the evidence the assessors have, they must make a judgement about any candidate's ability to thrive at the school.

The depth and capacity of feeling some former pupils have was brought home to me at Eton when I faced a difficult hour with an old-boy father as we discussed the expulsion of his son on a cannabis charge. I was treated to a damning analysis of the boy's house master and then of his own time at the school, which he had hated. Rather to my relief the conversation ended and he left through my secretary's office. After a few moments he reappeared around my door: 'Head Master,' he said, 'given everything that has happened, I think we should talk about the choice of house for my younger son.' This apparent desire to inflict equal pain across the family may be seen as one of those peculiarly English traits, but it may also illustrate an ability on the part of both parent and school to treat each child individually according to their needs. In this case, the younger son came into the school and was successful.

School admission, it should be said, is a minefield for every head. In the independent sector there is either the fall-out from being over-subscribed or the sleepless nights that come with chasing the market to fill places. State school heads wrestle with local authority policies and the growth industry that is the process of appealing against heads' decisions. One way or another, admissions take up significant time.

Despite the awkwardness around admissions and some wonderfully intemperate criticism, the loyalty and support of old boys can be a valuable thing. There is a temptation to assume that, as if by definition, all former pupils are destined to be backswoodsmen, locked in to the past or driven by self-interest, but many wish to see their school adapting to the times and being a leading rather than a following school. I have been struck and pleasantly surprised by the well of support offered by old boys at Eton for the provision of bursaries for talented boys from less advantaged backgrounds to enable them to have the benefit of an education that they themselves had enjoyed.

Fund-raising

Over the past quarter of a century, fund-raising has become fully a part of the language of headship. When I started as a head it would have been felt rather *de trop* to talk about such things as regular giving and fund-raising. An appeal for money would only be made in respect of a specific project, a sports hall for example, with all the money raised going expressly to that end. More recently it has become evident that an American-style approach to consistent giving can be hugely beneficial to schools, including state schools, some of which have been effective in raising money to supplement their income. Fund-raising as a practice and a state of mind is here to stay.

The Americans are often cited as being a culture apart in this respect and it is certainly true that well-established operations at top schools and universities in the USA have been staggeringly successful. Eton and Christ's Hospital are the two British schools with the largest endowments, but in per capita terms these endowments are about one-quarter of the American equivalent. Harvard is now truly needs-blind, able to offer places on merit without regard to the ability of parents to pay fees, such is the large pot of bursary money available to it.

It is wrong, however, to assume that the British are altogether new to the party. A walk around an historic school will reveal plaques to generous benefactors whose names appear on buildings, sometimes in a bold and unembarrassed way stating the exact amount of donated money alongside. The Edwardians and Victorians and their forebears gave a great deal. It was two World Wars and the Depression that effectively bankrupted the country and turned off the tap. These benefactions largely seemed to go out of fashion. It has taken a post-Thatcher generation, used to free-flowing markets, to restore a readiness to give and it is a generation seemingly less interested in bricks and mortar and more focused on bursaries.

In Eton's case, over six million pounds was able to be spent in 2014, with some 270 boys receiving substantial financial help averaging two-thirds remission of the fee. All applications for bursaries are means-tested and 70 receive full fee remission, by happy chance mirroring the 70 places for 'poor and indigent Scholars' which were part of Henry VI's foundation in 1440. Offering financial support on a major scale is a shift of gear for Eton as it is for many independent schools, and while being 'needs blind' is still some way off, it is a realistic aim.

Fund-raising, and the nurturing of relationships to support it, will loom larger in heads' eyes. Glancing across to America we see heads for whom their primary function is 'development', which is the Anglo-Saxon euphemism for 'raising money'. It is possible to envisage British heads becoming consumed by the demands of development, possibly to the detriment of their role as educational leaders. It will be a task for the next generation to strike a balance.

Local communities

Another dimension or constituency that will continue to be a challenge for heads is the broader local community. Some of the largest boarding schools can dominate their towns or villages, offering significant economic and cultural benefits to the local community, but living cheek-by-jowl with any institution, especially one of teenagers, can bring its own problems. More than once I have found myself with a bouquet of flowers in hand knocking at someone's door in a block of flats at the end of town, there to apologize for the boorish and/or drunken behaviour of a group of pupils who had slunk off to the pub next door. The difficulty is that while the vast majority of school pupils in most schools are polite and considerate most of the time, the handful that are not manage to strut their stuff in the most public of places at the most inopportune of moments. One parent of a prospective pupil told me that her son was Eton-bound despite her family living close to another well-known school, not, I discovered, to give the boy the opportunity to experience the glories of Eton, but to get him away from the loutish behaviour of their neighbouring school. The school to which she referred is a very good school: she lived too close.

The traffic is not all one-way. Heads can be irritated by the assumptions made by some local people that they are owed free access to school facilities when they wish or have a right to drive at speed through the middle of the school.

John Buchanan, the great pioneering head master of Oakham School, once described local affairs in Rutland as developing a 'Sophoclean intensity'. I have had occasion to recall that phrase when I have been the recipient of ill-concealed anger over pupil protests at alleged price rigging in a high-street shop or teenage ineptitude at crossing the road or smokers using the same lock-up garage down by the bridge. There is a permanent rumble of issues of some kind, yet set against the complaints are expressions of gratitude – for the choir's contribution to a charity service or to boys who made a real effort to be effective mentors in a local school, or to pupils who went out of their way to help a stranger find their destination.

Helping young people to become useful citizens is a large part of what good schools are trying to achieve. It is not always obvious to teenagers that the theory and rhetoric with which they are familiar should translate into sympathetic, positive action on the high street, but they learn. Some will only learn through making mistakes, and as a head I am all too aware it is sometimes a school's local community that bears the brunt of it.

Governors

Overarching all these constituencies is the school's governing body. I was surprised when I first became a head to discover that the HMC (Head Masters Conference), which

I had understood was the body that represented the top two hundred or so independent schools, did not represent the schools at all but was a members' organization, in effect a trades union. Founded in 1869 by the high-minded Dr Thring of Uppingham with a dozen or so fellow heads to discuss matters of education of the moment, HMC has developed a significant voice in national education but it has also been the backstop for beleaguered heads. Over the years it has been extraordinary to witness, fortunately at a distance, the pettiness, lack of vision and sheer incompetence of some governing bodies. In this regard there could be little to choose between independent and state schools – it seems a matter of serendipity whether a school is well governed.

It is not difficult to find tales of misgovernance, especially in relationship to the head: a head facing sustained criticism over time is sacked by his new chairman a week into the new academic year, an action destined to cause maximum stress for all involved including parents and pupils; a head's relationship with his chairman deteriorates to the point that communication is only conducted through written notes; a split governing body appoints one man as head only to sack him before he takes up his appointment in favour of another; the governing body believing in robust interrogation of candidates discovers that the entire shortlist for the post of head has melted away leaving them with nobody; or the governors who whimsically reject the best candidate in the field because he has a beard.

Governing bodies need to nurture their heads, giving them critical oversight but offering constructive advice, too, and recognizing that the head's role can be a lonely one. I was particularly grateful to a couple of governors in my first headship who went out of their way to look after the new head and his wife socially and who took an interest in us as a family. In return, heads need to keep their governing bodies well informed; a governor should never find out something, especially a criticism, from another source. So too, in providing written information, some governors prefer succinct summaries, others want copious detail. Part of the head's job is to help educate his own governing body about what really matters in school life, which may not be at all evident to someone from another walk of life, however distinguished they may be.

The head needs to be responsive to all queries, whatever they are (I once had to explain to a local-authority-appointed governor what A Levels were) and open in his dealings with governors, welcoming them into the school whenever they wish. When a head requests help it should be taken seriously. The daily, unsettling and unsolicited ministry of a local clergyman (and governor) at the teachers' mid-morning break stopped abruptly when the splendidly direct chairman drew the line.

Structures of governance vary considerably. Eton is unique in having two full-time residential governors (the Chairman and Vice-Chairman) on site, living either side of the Head. Fellow heads blanch at the prospect when they hear of it and it is not a formula likely to emerge from modern management consultation, carrying as it does opportunities for misunderstanding and crossed lines, but it works if the people involved want to make it work, showing respect for the other position. And that is the bottom line about governance. Training of governors tends to focus on responsibilities and systems, but it is the human dimension, understanding, courtesy and support, that matter most.

These constituencies form the broader school community. For a head, giving each of them the time they might wish is an impossibility and heads develop their own distinctive style. Some will feel they are the managerial type, others that they are pastorally 'there for the pupils', others that they are first and foremost trainers and motivators of staff. In truth, a head needs to be all these things. It is a job for people who enjoy range and variety and an often unpredictable day; people for whom the art of plate spinning is attractive.

Time

For some years I was asked by HMC, as an experienced head, to talk to new heads about time management, and how to deal with an array of competing demands. I became well versed in the theory. I would speak about such things as time logs, the subtle art of delegation, 'smart' goals and protocols for email. I was also able to pass on a few practical tips, like dealing with the daily influx of paper by standing next to a bin and rigorously using that receptacle for filing the unnecessary. I knew the received wisdom of the workplace that not more than 60 per cent of office time should be allocated to meetings. Yet while I was able to talk with some confidence about taming the pressures and bending the numerous demands to my will, I rarely was able to practise what I preached. It was too easy to be trapped in an office, harder to be out and about watching, listening and participating. Geography plays a part; at Chigwell my study overlooked a central area through which large numbers of teachers and pupils would pass during the day, so that a great many conversations were conducted on the staircase or in the courtyard; at Eton, which is on a much larger site, there proved to be no equivalent opportunity, so I needed to be more structured in my use of time to ensure that I had regular contact with the people who mattered most: the pupils.

I found it helpful to have the first half-hour of the morning, before the official start of the day at 8.30 a.m. available to any boy who wished to see me without appointment. It took a while for the habit to become established, but on average three or four boys would come each day with a range of motives, from the signing of a prize voucher to a disingenuous attempt to have me overturn a decision taken by their house master. There would be surprises, too, a boy appearing with a sophisticated plan to work the stock market in conjunction with pupils from a local state school with the intention of raising money for charity, or the boy who came to say that he had written to the Dalai Lama asking for an audience, which had been granted on condition the boy's head master went with him (we did; it was a remarkable experience). The second pupil-focused routine of the day was dealing with disciplinary matters personally each day: on reflection there is no better way to stay in touch with the narrative of the school day and I regret not being engaged in this way at my previous schools. The third was social and a regular pleasure; my wife and I would have all the senior boys in groups for lunch in our house.

Together with the daily mid-morning meeting with the teaching staff, often the busiest time of the day with many issues dealt with swiftly and face to face, these routine points in the diary created the framework on which everything else was hung.

As many heads would say, it has been a working life with many meetings and too little time for reflection; meetings about curriculum change, the financing of bursaries, provision of care for mental health, strategic planning for building development, meetings about IT infrastructure and development of software, about remuneration packages and conditions of service. There were collective meetings with house masters, Heads of Departments and Committees of every stripe; individual meetings with teachers; meetings with delegations from schools, education departments and governments from around the world; meetings at their request with parents about any issue (in how many companies would the chief executive be readily accessible to any customer?) and always, when they asked, meetings with pupils.

It leads to long and full days made longer by the likelihood of almost all evenings being taken up with a function or event of some kind; a play or a concert, a staff gathering, an old-boy event, society meetings organized by boys or some other meeting that could not be fitted into daylight hours. The mail is checked over lunch, correspondence dealt with late at night. These are fulfilling, satisfying days as long as fitness and health are good. A prime attribute for any head is stamina. To see heads labouring with their duties under the yoke of illness is sad indeed and it is often the case that they must do so with little support. Heads are simply meant to get on with it.

There are bad days, of course, usually a consequence of someone in the school letting everyone down. Discovering, for example, that a senior teacher had failed to mark homework for a whole term and that this had not been picked up by normal processes but had come to light when, after far too long, pupils complained; the sense of collective failure at such a moment is palpable. Bad days come, too, when an outside agency causes an unnecessary waste of time. In 2005, the Office of Fair Trading initiated an investigation, prompted by headline-grabbing coverage in a national newspaper, of alleged fee fixing in independent schools. It was true that bursars in independent schools had for many years been in the habit of asking about likely fee increases, the knowledge gained having the effect of holding back fee rises as no one wished to be too far ahead. It was also true that the law had changed and schools were unaware of it. It was a technical infringement which could have been dealt with swiftly with a slap on the wrist and a signpost to better practice. In fact the investigation led to months of debate and cost until, finally, a formula was worked out that was agreed to be the least bad option. The whole business was a nonsense, a good illustration of the insensitive hand of bureaucracy creating a beast that must be fed.

The growth of bureaucracy has been a distinct feature of my time as a head. Although in a smaller school than Eton, I started as a head with one secretary and the bursar also had a secretary. There was a small buildings team run by a clerk of works. As I finish as a head, I work with an HR department (the term itself alien to long-standing teachers), copious numbers operating in Finance, a large Works department and not one but two full-time Health and Safety officials. In each case, the necessity for the appointment of an additional person in the area of regulation and compliance has been well made. Under a welter of legislation, much of it worthwhile in intent, schools have had to become more like professional businesses. This change has brought with it a welcome awareness of the realities faced by companies generally, and schools are rightly not exempt from workplace legislation such as the effects of change to retirement horizons or safety-at-work rules, but it is a change that has caused a shift in culture.

Teachers are wary, worried that taking a school trip overseas or even at home will bring too much hassle and the risk of legal action being taken against them. They worry too about the implicit dangers of being alone in a room with a child, however strong the pastoral need, because their action might be misinterpreted. And they are wary of conversations they have with parents and sometimes with pupils, which the agents of good practice say should be noted and logged at every turn. All those involved with managing a school need to be wary of 'the forces of tidiness', the urge to apple-pie order when it is unnecessary. All schools need to be on their guard against a rising tide of faceless formality which threatens to drown intuitive human responses to situations involving other human beings.

In a community in which people live in close proximity and days are busy, there are inevitably moments of tension, with tempers exploding or unresolved festering antipathies finding fierce expression in an unexpected way – and that is true of both adults and the young. It remains reassuring, however, that the tide of school life runs remarkably smoothly, testimony to the purposeful examples set by many and the desire to make things work. A boarding environment teaches everyone within it to get on with people to whom they are not necessarily drawn: getting on with people you like is easy.

Testing moments tend to be sparked when something or someone from outside the school strikes the match. Protesters on the street, whether wannabe anarchists or anti-hunt activists or the simply unintelligible, cause a ripple of interest which can pose a challenge to the school during a working day. It is one thing to encourage pupils to see protest as a right in a democracy, but another to persuade them not to respond energetically and physically (as they are sometimes provoked to do). It is not easy when you are 16 to stand back and realize that not responding can be more powerful than playing someone else's game.

The bizarre should never surprise a head. Lunch with a group of boys was interrupted by my secretary, who called me away to deal with an incident. A man, claiming to be a human bomb, had kidnapped one of the school doctors by the entrance to the medical centre. By the time I arrived, the school head of security had shown remarkable courage in approaching and facing up to the man. After quite some while, the man started to talk and released his hostage. He was a poor, sick soul wearing a brick not a bomb. As I had been standing outside the police cordon unable to elicit any information, my mobile phone rang. It was a journalist from a national tabloid, who told me exactly who the man was and asked for a comment. It struck me then that if I were ever to need information in difficult circumstances I should always ask a tabloid journalist. I was also struck that, as the word spread, most of the school knew something was afoot but the boys were sensible and got on with their lives. There was no evidence of 'Eton boys in their tailcoats running for their lives' that appeared in some news reports the next day.

The outside world

Dealing with intrusion from the outside world, especially from the media, is a distinctive facet of the head's role at Eton. Media interest always runs high. I doubt there can be another secondary school in the world where the appellation 'old boy' labels a former pupil for life: even octogenarians will still be described as old Etonians, neatly pinning them with a tag that seems self-evidently to capture a social caricature, a character type and world view. That Eton celebrates being rather a mixed bag of individuals and is arguably less posh than some other schools is neither here nor there; the label sticks. This desire to pigeon-hole is a constant presence in the mind of the Head. On occasion, I have found myself running headlines in my head as I have been dealing with situations. I hope I have had the strength of character to deal honestly and properly with all situations that have come my way but the public angle is always there, rustling in the shadows.

There were times in my previous schools when I wondered what it would take to arouse any press interest at all in my school. Nothing quite prepares a head for having to deal with 20 different media contacts about an incident in the space of two hours. It would be easy to become defensive or sound paranoid about press intrusions, but in truth a high level of media interest cuts both ways.

On the debit ticket are the comic misrepresentations – '100 guns found in Eton padre's rooms' turned out to be a garbled account of a standard police check on the CCF armoury then run, as it happened, by a school chaplain. There are also the occasions when families are unfairly exposed to the public glare. An incident involving three 14-year-old boys illicitly purchasing vodka, drinking on the school playing fields and behaving boorishly with some girls should be the stuff of an investigation and disciplinary sanction, but not a story for the front page of a serious national newspaper. Nor is it always straightforward having a story published as discussed: a balanced piece about the school's carefully nuanced drugs policy, written by an assiduous young journalist, becomes sub-edited with the nuance removed and under a provocative headline.

A shorthand sloppy approach to journalism has also given Eton undue praise. When a local man was appointed to look after Muslim boys for their act of worship in lieu of Sunday chapel, this was a story that was embellished ('Eton's first Imam') and went global. Eton came across as forward-thinking and inclusive. As it turned out, the appointment proved very good for the boys and the school community. I was subsequently asked by an admiring

MP who had pitched that story for us – it had needed no pitching, it developed a life of its own.

For all the irritating sloppiness and misrepresentation, however, much of the coverage has been fair or merited. It is right that there should be public scrutiny of the privilege surrounding a place like Eton, its commitment to public benefit in relation to charitable status, for example. It is right that the press should publish stories broadly in the public interest. Sometimes the school's profile can help forward an educational argument (about the fragility of public examination marking, for example). All schools, even schools like Eton, that face potential pitfalls in media terms must be open and stay connected with public interest. All schools, even Eton, are part of our national story of education.

For all the workload and frustrations, there have been wonderful moments. There is no better satisfaction than seeing young people achieve remarkable things: the 17-year-old who takes the initiative and organizes a distinguished panel of economists to speak to 500 sixth-formers from dozens of independent and state schools; the boy who inspires, organizes and conducts a full-scale performance of the Brahms *Requiem*; the girl who writes and produces her own play. Just as satisfying are the moments when a teenager turns a corner; the wayward, irritating 14-year-old boy becomes the 17-year-old speaking with sober clarity about his ambition to join the army; the spikey, truculent, unhappy 14-year-old girl becomes the reliable prefect with a gift for helping younger children.

There is great satisfaction, too, in seeing the germ of an idea become a matter of substance in the life of the school. Some of these developments are headline news, such as a major change to the curriculum, but many are under the bonnet, small changes that cumulatively make a difference. I am happy to admit that almost all the good ideas have come from the great people around me. Working with highly committed, capable teachers has been a continuing delight.

I have also been fortunate in being supported in three headships by my wife. An accomplished teacher herself, she has chosen to take an interest in the school community in many unsung but effective ways. A quarter of a century ago this was rather expected: today she is as likely to face criticism from other women for not having her own full-time career as quiet appreciation. Yet school communities need her, and people like her, more than ever before. Community needs to be sustained by commitment and replenished every day or it slowly dies.

In the end, for both of us, our prime motivation is simple, old-fashioned and unremarkable. We see what we do as service, service to the young who continue to inspire us with their optimism, energy and hope.

It is a wonderful job.

14

Ten Questions that Need Answers

These are the questions I would ask when considering a school for my child. They are not questions with pat answers and take some teasing out. If the answers are brisk or bland, be suspicious. These are questions that go to the heart of what makes a good school.

In many cases the best way to find an answer is to ask around. Beware parents with a gripe or grudge, but take in a range of people and opinion. No school can get everything right, or even mostly right. Schools are intricate organisms with many moving parts. On a good day, most of the parts are moving in the right direction. It is particularly on a bad day that you can test whether a school has the vision and the heart to deal with its pupils honestly, fairly and with respect.

1. Does the school genuinely root its culture in good relationships?

This is a very different thing from front-of-house charm. Is eye contact good when you walk around the school? Both pupils and adults? Do teachers greet each other readily and warmly? Do pupils feel they matter? How are they dealt with when they are in trouble? Do former pupils come back and visit?

2. Is there an evident commitment to an all-round education?
Is the school driven and dominated by exam results? Is the co-curriculum built in to the structure of the week, or is it merely extra? Does spiritual life matter as much as rugby?

3. Does the head inspire confidence?
Schools are communities and often work as a team, but the person at the top has significant impact on the direction and tone of the school. Does the head enable teachers to do a proper job or is s/he a control freak? Do pupils know who the head is when s/he walks around the school (this is not as daft a question as it may sound)? Does the head have presence: is there a moment of respectful recognition when s/he enters a classroom? Is the head a systems person or does s/he work through the people around him?

4. Is the school committed to the continuing professional development of its teachers?

Does the head talk about the education of teachers as well as pupils when s/he is on the stump selling the school? Is there written evidence readily available to show how training is part of the warp and weft of school life?

5. Are the teachers inspiring?
Do parents come away from parents' meetings feeling that they have been speaking to switched-on people with a vocation? Do they feel the teachers really know their child and their subject? Do they feel grateful and supported when a teacher is critical about their child?

6. Do the facilities facilitate?
Most schools have glossy brochures. They do not always convey the reality (one gave prominence to a photo of floodlit astro-turf facilities which turned out to be at another school!) Even if the theatre is state-of-the-art, what is the drama really like? It may be a multi-million-pound, architect-designed academy, but does it have enough classrooms? A shabby room with an old-fashioned blackboard can still be the home of great teaching.

7. Do the published statistics make any sense?
There is a bewildering array of statistics available these days. An adroit marketing person can 'prove' pretty much anything. Standardized tables of

inspection, such as government league tables, are more reassuring but should come with a very large health warning. What has been measured and how? Do shifts of percentage points mean anything? Would you want a school that is top of a league table anyway?

8. Is there time for pupils to experiment and also have time out?
There is a difference between being productively busy and busy for busy's sake. Does every minute of the school day have to be accounted for? Does the school value constructive play at whatever age? What opportunities are there for pupils to participate in things beyond their usual experience?

9. Can a young person learn to be his or her self?
Does the school expect conformity or prefer individuals in a community? Does the culture encourage pupils to tolerate difference and expect older pupils to take a lead and celebrate it? Are you invited to meet and talk with pupils? If you can, find a way to meet pupils away from school. They will reveal far more about their attitudes and about school culture when they are relaxed.

10. Does the school show off its institutional awards and badges?

If so, avoid. As a rule of thumb the display of
badges is in inverse proportion to the quality
of the school. And don't bother with the prospectus:
it will be lovely, but they all look the same.
Trust your instinct!

Having interrogated potential schools, and in the spirit
of honesty and reciprocity, there follow the 10 questions
I would wish parents should ask of themselves if
considering my school:

1. Do I believe my child is almost perfect?

2. Do I like rules and regulations until my child breaks
   them?

3. Am I happy gossiping about the school to anyone
   who will listen, but reluctant to talk to the head?

4. Do I go in at the deep end when someone criticizes my
   child?

5. Am I an expert because I went to school myself?

If the answer to any of the above is 'yes', please find another
school.

6. Am I prepared to work with the school and pull my
   weight?

7. Can I strike a balance between being a Velcro parent
   and a ghost?

8. Can I support my child and support the school
   through difficult times?

9. Can I suppress my frustrated ambitions and let my child be herself?

10. Will I deflect rumour and find out the facts from the school?

If the answer to any one of questions 6–10 is 'yes', welcome. We will be able to work with you and your child will flourish.

ACKNOWLEDGEMENTS

First and foremost my thanks go to Amanda Mannering for her patience and perseverance, not least in cajoling a busy head to find time to focus on writing : like any good teacher, she has sought to keep me up to the mark. So, too, Robin Baird-Smith who suggested the book in the first place.

Colleagues from my own school and from many others have helped shape the way I have come to think about education. One of the joys of a lifetime in teaching has been witnessing the professional quality and profound vocation of some highly gifted individuals. Of the many colleagues who have influenced me, too many to mention, the following have helped in some way with this book: Gerard Evans, Will Evans, Robin Fletcher, Percy Harrison, Jay Lakhani, Paul McAteer, Jonnie Noakes, Ciran Stapleton, Bob Stephenson and Keith Wilkinson. Many thanks also to Martina Prentis and Jeanne Nanda for their continuing support.

And, not least, I thank the generations of pupils who have inspired me, not least my daughter, Sophie. Some of them I have come across again as parents attempting, in their turn, to make sense of their adolescent children. It seems a familiar pattern but we are all, mercifully, idiosyncratically different – and that difference has been a constant fascination and cause for celebration.

FURTHER READING

This list is deliberately short. Books about education abound and it would be all too easy to offer a library of further reading. I have been influenced by many writers, sometimes directly, but more often than not by phrases and ideas that have seeped into my consciousness and shaped my thinking. What follows are some books that have caused me to think afresh. Their ideas, often based on thorough research, push back some of the boundaries we have erected around teaching and learning. If there is a common theme, it is explaining what is meant by 'educating the whole child' and why this is so crucial for all of us.

To begin with, my touchstone in this book is:

A. C. Benson, *The Schoolmaster* (Woodbridge: Peridot Press, 2011; first published 1902).

The best account I have read written by a teacher about the business of teaching is:

Jonathan Smith, *The Learning Game* (London: Little, Brown, 2000).

Of heavier weight, but great inspiration, are books that demonstrate the rich variety of ways we learn and learn about learning:

Howard Gardner, *Frames of Mind: the Theory of Multiple Intelligences* (New York: Basic Books, 1983).

Martin Seligman, *Learned Optimism* (New York: Knopf, 1999).

Carol Dweck, *Mindset: the New Psychology of Success* (New York: Random House, 2006).

Bill Lucas and Guy Claxton, *Educating Ruby: What our Children Really Need to Learn* (Carmarthen: Crown House, 2015)

Perhaps of less general interest, but valuable for those who find themselves in a classroom:

John Hattie, *Visible Learning for Teachers: Maximising Impact on Learning* (London: Routledge, 2012).

Ron Berger, *An Ethic of Excellence: Building a Culture of Craftsmanship into Students* (New York: Heinemann, 2003).

Doug Lemov, *Teach Like a Champion: 49 Techniques that Put Students on the Path to College* (San Francisco: Jossey-Bass, 2010).

Ian Warwick and Martin Stephen, *Educating the More Able Student* (Los Angeles: Sage, 2015).

To find out something more about Europe's most successful education system:

Pasi Sahlberg, *Finnish Lessons: What can the World Learn from Educational Change in Finland?* (New York: Teachers College Press, 2011).

On imagination and teaching:

David Whyte, *The Teacher's Vocation* (Washington: Many Rivers, 2001).

It is often through fiction that one comes closest to the heart of things. Schools, however, are ill-served. It is hard to capture relationships between children and teenagers in a way that seems real. School stories tend to be caricatures from jolly hockey sticks to hard knocks. However, one of the best insights into what it is like to feel a disconnected, unheard teenager remains J. D. Salinger's, *The Catcher in the Rye* (London: Penguin, 1989). Perhaps oddly, it is the fantasy world of Hogwarts and Harry Potter that captures something about friendship and trust.

When it comes to the adult world of teaching, there is a richer and more varied literature. In particular, the vocation of teaching is explored in different ways by:

Muriel Spark, *The Prime of Miss Jean Brodie* (London: Penguin, 2000).

James Hilton, *Goodbye Mr Chips* (London: Pilot Books, 1952).

E. R. Braithwaite, *To Sir with Love* (London: New Windmills, 1971).